Tales of the Wild

A Year With Nature

With Foreword by Sam Robbins

To Sandy,
It was fun having you in our
Bjorklunden Class. *Best Wishes,*
Charlotte Lukes
Sept. 12, 2019

by Roy Lukes

Cover Photo: Cave Point (photographed by Roy Lukes)

First Edition
First Printing, 2000

Front Cover (Cave Point), Inside Front Cover (Northern Goshawk)
        and Inside Back Cover Photographs: Roy Lukes
Back Cover Photograph (Roy and Ruffed Grouse): Charlotte Lukes
Snow Crystal Photograph: W. A. Bentley
All Other Story Photographs: Roy or Charlotte Lukes
Book Design: Roy and Charlotte Lukes, Nature-Wise.
Pre-press Composition: Laddie Chapman.
Foreword: Samuel D. Robbins Jr.
Printing: Van Lanen Printing Co., Inc., Green Bay, Wisconsin.

ISBN 0-9665181-1-X (softcover)
Library of Congress Card Number: 99-091360

For more information contact the publishers at:
Nature-Wise
Roy and Charlotte Lukes
Post Office Box 105
Egg Harbor, Wisconsin 54209-0105

Contents

Foreword

Introduction

January *1*

Sublime Frosty Memories *2*
Skyline Pine *7*
Brush Pile Philosophy *9*
White Paradise.................................. *13*
Merlin, The Magician *16*

February................... *21*

Frigid Feathered Friends *22*
Lady Of The Woods........................ *26*
The Snowflake Man *30*
Cold Feet, Warm Heart.................... *34*
Tacamahac Trees *38*

March *43*

Favorite Stone Fences *44*
Tree Silhouettes *49*
I'm Taking A Lichen To You............ *51*
In Defense Of Crows *57*
Frail Children Of The Air *61*

April.......................... *65*

The Sweet Sugar Maple *66*
Chippie.. *70*
Thoreau And Earth Day *74*
Drum And Bugle Corps *78*
April Warm-Up *80*

May........................... *87*

White Star Of The Woods............... *88*
Wildflower Parade *92*
Master Carpenter............................. *96*
Red-Eyed Minstrels *99*
Fearless Plover *103*

June 107

Slow But Snappy 108
Our Summer Squirrel 111
Winged Jewels 115
Fabulous Ferns 119
Night Wings 122

July 127

Playing Possum 128
A Honey Of A Tree 132
Flowers' Gentle Partners 135
Snakes Alive! 140
Water Your Birds! 145

August 149

Phantom Of The Woods 150
Lacy Umbrellas 153
The Voiceless Singer 156
Spot The Amphibian 159
Big Daddy Stiltwalker 163

September 167

Insect Houdini 168
Needle-Billed Dynamos 171

Doll's Eyes 175
A Caterpillar, Dressed 178
Woodland Drummer 183

October 189

Nature's Spirals 190
Ancient Tree Of Life 194
The Golden Conifers 199
Acorns And Oaks 202
Ruby Of The Muskeg 205

November 211

Praying For Prey 212
The Cosmopolitan Fruit 217
Woody Recyclers 220
Seeds Of Life 224
Little Wise Guy 229

December 233

White-Tailed Moochers 234
Fragrant Spires 238
"Butterflies" Of Winter 242
The Christmas Bird 246
Commune With Nature 250

Index 255

Foreword

Just think! Roy Lukes has been writing newspaper articles for 32 years—almost a third of a century. How many readers in the Door County, Green Bay and Appleton region have expanded their knowledge and appreciation of nature by reading Roy's articles is impossible to estimate.

It is considerable, if I am to judge by the mail I have received from 22 years of writing bird-related articles for "The Country Today." Yes, like Roy, I am a naturalist, and proud to be one. But my columns have all been about birds. My knowledge of ferns and flowers, of chipmunks and chorus frogs, of potatoes and 'possums, of tamaracks and turtles leave much to be desired. Were I to tackle birches and brushpiles, or spiders and squirrels, they might be subtitled "confusions of a naturalist." Under Roy's hand these sixty essays blossom as "confessions of a naturalist."

The author has a keen eye for both the familiar and the unfamiliar. Not only does he describe the well-known distraction display of a parent killdeer defending its nest, but also he interprets the less-frequently seen "roll-over" defense used by the hog-nosed snake. Once while attending an outdoor concert, offered by two musicians against a background of flowering potentilla bushes, Roy was distracted by a dorcas copper butterfly that seemed to dance among the potentilla blossoms as the musicians sang.

I detect four sources of inspiration that drew Roy into his dual life as naturalist at the Ridges Sanctuary and as the author of nature-oriented books and newspaper columns. (1) A camera. This was a graduation gift from discerning parents. Cameras are a part of every household, but few people have used cameras as effectively as Roy in entering into the lives of spores, buds, birds, insects, ice crystals and snowflakes. (2) Jim Zim. Even before I encountered the name Jim

Zimmerman in Roy's introduction, I caught a glimpse of Jim in the titles of these essays. During his lifetime Jim Zim (he lived but four blocks from my home) was encyclopedic in his knowledge of the integral relationships of animals and plants. (3) A nature-oriented public. What newspaper editor could afford to keep one of his columnists for 30+ years without strong support from his readers? (4) Wife Charlotte. Some wives assist their husbands by typing their manuscripts. Charlotte has done much more: adding her insights as they hike together, sketching natural and unnatural scenes, and sharing with Roy the esthetics Mother Nature has in store for all of us.

May all who read "Tales of the Wild" cultivate that same sense of wonder and appreciation!

— *Sam Robbins*

Introduction

It was in early June of 1956, having completed my first year of teaching at the Shorewood Hills School in Madison, Wisconsin, that I participated in a week-long learning experience that changed my life. A notice in one of Madison's daily newspapers told of a "Reading The Landscape" outdoor education class for teachers to be conducted by Dr. James Zimmerman – Jim as we all came to call him.

Our group of around a dozen met early each morning at the Madison School Forest near Verona where some of our classes were held. Various nearby environments, including a quaking bog, prairie, marsh, typical roadsides and several kinds of woods were explored under Jim's excellent guidance and incredibly wonderful interpretation.

Little did we students realize at the time what a learned and skilled field biologist Jim was. It was the interrelationships between soil, plants, insects, birds, mammals, climate and other factors that were so meaningfully taught and explained. The identification of birds, their songs and some of their call notes were highlighted and reflected Jim's outstanding command of this subject.

His knowledge of plants, their names and fascinating stories about them, how and by which insects they were pollinated, for example, were tied in beautifully with the functioning of a healthy ecosystem. "Hands on" learning about the Great Outdoors came alive for us that week as we hiked, sat, listened, observed, examined and, in short, were thoroughly turned on to the natural world surrounding us.

A vital feature of the week was Jim's stressing the importance of continuous, on-going learning about nature through the seasons, becoming our own best teachers, the use of reference materials, and the great and long-lasting benefits of good communication.

I shall always be deeply indebted to my parents for the guidance and good family discipline and work ethics they taught me, and especially for encouraging and trusting me to spend countless hours, as a boy growing up in Kewaunee, canoeing on the river, hiking and exploring the river bottoms, swamps, fields, and beaches along Lake Michigan.

My folks' gift to me of a 35-mm camera upon graduating from the Door-Kewaunee Normal School in 1951 sparked my interest in nature photography which has continued and grown during the past 48 years. "Several" cameras later, along with a few thousand black and white negatives, photographs, and colored transparencies, I have learned what a useful tool photography can be in teaching and writing about Nature.

Undoubtedly inspired by my great friend and Mentor, Jim Zimmerman, I met with Chandler Harris, editor at the time of the *Door County Advocate*, in June of 1968 to discuss the possibility of writing weekly nature stories for that bi-weekly paper. My first story appeared in the July 20, 1968 edition. Today, 31 years and 1740 essays later, as I read over the first paragraph of that nature essay, I strongly feel that the message I hoped my readers would accept as a challenge and put into practice then is exactly the same as I would try to instill in them now.

I wrote, "Rarely does nature fail to produce some thrilling experiences for those who take to the out-of-doors, are eager to learn, and are willing to be patient and observant. Door County, rich in native plants and animals, is an ideal classroom for such experiences. People who learn to understand and enjoy our natural resources will not be satisfied unless they can repeat these experiences year after year. And if many people develop this noble attitude, our beautiful county will stand a chance of remaining beautiful – and perhaps even improve its natural condition."

Having written nature stories for newspapers for a long time, and taken many hundreds of black and white photographs with which to illustrate them, one eventually realizes that certain ones have become favorites. Either I have received many kind words from readers regarding these special essays, or the experiences upon which the stories were based are pleasantly memorable and will live with Charlotte and me forever. Even the photographs, mostly taken by me, a few by Charlotte, and the incredible and historical snow crystal microphotograph by W.A. Bentley, played an important role in selecting the stories.

I have chosen, in putting together this fifth book, *Tales of the Wild, A Year With Nature*, 60 of my favorite stories, five for each month of the year. Included are some about birds, mammals, trees, stone fences, snow crystals, wildflowers, ferns, frogs, mushrooms, butterflies and others. They invariably are quite easily found subjects. All that must be done is to "look around you!"

I give special thanks to the *Door County Advocate*, the *Appleton Post-Crescent*, and the *Green Bay Press-Gazette* for having first published the essays, contained in this book and covering a span of 27 years, and for giving me their wholehearted support in putting some of them into seasonal story form in *Tales of the Wild, A Year With Nature*.

Phone calls and letters from many readers of my weekly nature essays have directed me to their outstanding discoveries of various plants and animals which, in turn, frequently led to photographs and stories. These alert observers of the natural world around them are greatly appreciated.

Lastly I give my heartfelt thanks to Charlotte my wife, for her unending encouragement and inspiration, for her valuable input along with proofreading, correcting and improving my stories, creating titles for the essays, making the index, and for the many hours spent in being my most favorite and best "Partner In Nature!"

— *Roy Lukes*

January

Sublime Frosty Memories

Even though this has been one of the mildest and snowless Decembers of the past 50 years, recent mornings have produced exquisite displays of frost crystals. Our predawn arisings are rewarded with wonderful and memorable shows of these delicate white traceries.

One of the most fascinating discoveries I've ever had following a good old-fashioned blizzard came when I was sweeping the snow off the windshield of our 1976 van. There, just waiting to be appreciated, were hundreds of ornate ice "flowers" and dainty white "Tannenbaums" formed in their matchless delicacy on the inner surface of the glass. Our good friend, Jack Frost, had produced another artistic masterpiece. Apparently the amount of trapped water vapor and the subtle changes of air temperature during the night had been ideal.

Frost forms best outdoors or in unheated rooms. Fortunately for us, water vapor is invisible. We can see it only in its liquid or solid state. When the water content of the air is low, such as in winter, lips and hands easily become chapped. In fact there is about six times more moisture present at 86 degrees F. than at 32 degrees F.

A memorable experience as a youngster was awakening on a subzero morning in the large upstairs bedroom where I slept with my three brothers, Ivan, Leo and Richard. The hot air

I thank my lucky "snow stars and frost crystals" that one of my sixth grade teachers, Doris Shubert, taught us some of the great literary masters' poems. One of my favorites, that I continue to enjoy each winter, is John Greenleaf Whittier's Snowbound. I distinctly remember drawing some pictures as a sixth grader to illustrate one of my most well-liked passages: "The old familiar sights of ours took marvelous shapes, strange domes and towers rose up where sty or corn-crib stood…"

register was usually closed and we awoke to find the three windows covered with crystalline forms, fairy forests of graceful hemlocks, spruces and firs, ferns and snow castles and all sorts of other imaginary wonders. We were never satisfied until we had pressed the tips of our tongues to the frosty scenes in order to melt tiny windows to the outdoor world.

Today, living as close to Lake Michigan as we do, we often awake to find nearly everything in sight outdoors temporarily coated with hoarfrost. This is formed by the passing of the invisible water vapor of the atmosphere into the ice crystal phase without going through the liquid state. The same principle occurs, but in reverse, when snow or ice evaporate directly into the atmosphere. This process is called sublimation.

One of the most elegant displays of plate-like hoarfrost took place in this region in February 1977. This unusual form of frost occurs in midwinter at low temperatures. Everything including weeds, barbed wire fences, shrubs and trees were trimmed with fragile, jagged, nickel-to-quarter-size, flat pointed discs of frost. I was so carried away with the astounding display that I came very close to freezing my fingers as I handled my icy cold cameras, snapping one picture after another. How I long for another experience like that in coming winters.

I can vividly recall a morning several years ago as quite a few people drove by our driveway at the old Rangelight Residence in Baileys Harbor. Some slowed down to stare in disbelief at me, balanced like a contortionist, near the top of the stepladder in front of our van's windshield. What they probably couldn't see was my camera and that I was photographing the perfectly formed window-glass frost. The temperature and light conditions were absolutely ideal, and I wasn't about to miss that chance.

I know someone, were he still alive and within sight, who would have clapped his hands and shouted in approval – Wilson A. Bentley, better known as "Snowflake Bentley."

This bachelor farmer-meteorologist from Jericho, Vermont became world-famous for his photographs of snowflakes taken through a microscope. Jericho is situated in northwest Vermont about 12 miles east of Lake Champlain in the foothills of the Green Mountains where it is not uncommon to receive 120 inches of snow in a winter.

Snowflake Bentley must have been a genuine individualist. Bored with school at an early age, he dropped out and his mother tutored him at home. He became quite an expert on the ferns of that region, learned to play the piano well and finally was turned on to his lifelong study of snow-flakes, frost and other weather phenomena. At age 15, he received a microscope for Christmas and, by trial and error, mastered the technique of photographing individual snow crystals at high magnification.

A favorite winter book in our library, *Snow Crystals,* by W. A. Bentley and W. J. Humphreys, published by Dover Publications, Inc., consists of 2,453 illustrations chosen from the 5,381 or more photographs of the astoundingly wonderful variety of snowflakes and related formations he took.

Every now and then life becomes far too serious and fast-paced to the point where a person has to allow his or her sense of imagination to help ease the tension. In other words, I'm perfectly content to let Jack Frost and his friends, the gnomes, decorate the windshield of our car at night – and chances are pretty good that I'll be teetering near the top of a stepladder the following morning enjoying and photographing their artwork!

The Skyline Pine stands vigil in our neighbors' field, a symbol of strength, beauty and perseverance. The tall white pine frequently serves as a perch on warm summer days to the Eastern Kingbird and American Kestrel, who both hunt for food in the surrounding meadow. The Eastern Meadowlark often chooses one of the pine's left uppermost branches from which to sing its rich, far-reaching song.

Skyline Pine

One of the most beautiful trees I ever knew ranks near the tops of two of my lists, the saddest and gladdest events of my life. We referred to the old battle scarred lonesome White Pine standing in an open field near the south end of Donald Hasenjager's farm south of Jacksonport simply as the "Hasenjager Pine."

What a monarch it was, lone sentinel of the skyline, standing silently in its appointed place. There in its fixed position, surrounded on all sides by fields, it miraculously endured insect attacks, massive breakage of one of the huge double trunks and many small branches, the burden of ice and snow, winds of gale force and especially the killing power of strike after strike of lightning.

That tree beckoned to me for a dozen or more years each time I drove by on my way to school or to Sturgeon Bay. Finally in August of 1975 a small group and I received permission to hike in to say "hello" to the monumental landmark. Its narrow irregularly shaped crown, looking for all the world like a giant Beaufort wind symbol on a weather map, showed signs of severe damage through the years.

Its apparent heroic proportions from a distance proved to be misleading. My clinometer indicated a height of about 60 feet. Nevertheless its total character, its great individuality, qualified it for everyone's list of favorites. So much for one of my gladdest events of that decade.

The morning of Friday, March 23, 1979 dawned warm and rainy. By nightfall the weather had turned windy and much colder. Gradually the rain changed to ice during the night and by morning the thermometer had sagged to 17 degrees F. It was snowing by Sunday.

Charlotte and I had to go into Sturgeon Bay Monday, March 26. Immediately after passing the Hasenjager farm we looked to the south to silently greet our old pine tree friend. I had to take a second look to believe what I was seeing. We both let out loud gasps! The pine was down! Nearly too stunned to drive or talk we reasoned that the high winds and freezing rain during the night of March 23 or early morning of the following day had felled the tree, one of my saddest events of the decade. Now photographs of the Hasenjager Pine would have to suffice.

One grandiose pine towering above the horizon is enough to establish a wonderful calming and cooling mood. We absolutely had to locate another accessible White Pine to take the place of our old fallen friend. It wasn't a planned discovery-type outing that led us to the new tree but rather an afternoon drive on Sunday, Oct. 30, 1977 to enjoy the day. A flock of Snow Buntings eating weed seeds between the rows of corn stubble first caught our attention along a lonely side road.

Eager for the next find we eased up the long gradual slope bounded closely by trees. Soon the roadsides opened as we approached one of the highest points of land in that part of Door County, and there it was. What a beauty of a White Pine, no larger than the other one, perhaps more symmetrical but about the same size trunk, a genuine guardian of this windswept panoramic and geological backbone. Eventually we realized that we could see the crown of this fine tree from about two and a half miles away towering over all the others, quite a standard-bearer of the horizon. This would be "our" Skyline Pine.

Quite a few of the tallest White Pines we have seen in recent years sported flattened tops. Frequently this is a sign of old age. Their terminal branches high above the ground are at the mercy of winter storms. It is their thick, bushy needle-foliage that accumulates so much weight during freezing rains or snowstorms. Then, followed by strong winds, much breakage occurs leaving the tree scarred with character for life. Tall flat-topped White Pines speak with authority, of muscling up to many vicious storms, unable to run for shelter, for 200 or more years.

Anthropomorphically, as an old monarch of a White Pine might say, "Do you see this big scar? That's where one of my best branches broke off during the terrible Armistice Day Blow of 1940!"

Today we view the Skyline Pine as a symbol of the new millennium to come, wondering what we can give in return to trees in general for what they give to us – wood products, fuel, recreational sites, watershed areas, erosion control, natural beauty, shade, oxygen, food and shelter for wildlife, lower summer air temperatures and a fine barrier to wind as well as man-made noises. The list goes on and on.

We look to the future with longing in our hearts for a more peaceful world more in tune and harmony with the land. The Skyline Pine will be our symbol of ages past when White Pines stood supreme. In fact we shall look often in the future to the old pine for inspiration. Even though silent, it speaks!

Brush Pile Philosophy

Several days ago I received a letter and two fine photographs from a reader telling of the strange white bird coming to their feeders. Its faint reddish forehead and yellow mandibles indicated that it most likely was a partial albino Common Redpoll. In my letter of reply I indicated how fortunate they were to have a naturally marked bird they could observe and enjoy from day to day knowing that it was the same creature.

The bird that we have admired so much this winter is a Dark-eyed Junco. All of the other migratory juncos left for the South well before the snow arrived, but for some reason this individual remained. Unlike the ordinary junco, this one has pinkish-tan sides. Several years ago, before so many birds received new names, it might have been referred to as a Pink-sided Junco.

A few weeks ago Charlotte was doing some work at the kitchen sink and happened to look into the woods east of the house at the perfect instant. Out of the brush pile on top of the glacial moraine flew the junco. Since that day, knowing about its hideout, we have watched our small friend come and go from its winter shelter many times.

On most days I put out bird food well before sunrise, often by 6 a.m. Then, as we eat, we enjoy recording the sequence of arrivals. The junco is always the first to appear along the edge of the yard for its breakfast of cracked corn and ground-up sunflower seeds.

Within several minutes of the pink-sided diner's arrival the Mourning Doves enter the scene like dark ghosts. They and the junco appear to get along extremely well. In fact it is common for the junco to be surrounded by the considerably larger doves, occasionally as many as 30.

My method of putting up firewood in our woods includes gathering and piling the brush. I do this for several reasons. In the first place the brush piles afford small mammals and birds good escape shelters from their natural predators. Secondly I enjoy studying, teaching about and photographing plants, insects and other facets of nature there and prefer to not have to stumble my way through the fallen brush.

When Charlotte and I cleared the thousand-foot-long corridor for our driveway through the woods on our property we had at least a dozen sizable brush piles along the route by the time we had completed the project. I remember hiking in along the opening that first fall before the driveway was built and watching several White-throated Sparrows flit ahead of us from one brush pile to the next.

As the human population increases and development of an area grows steadily, the landscape can get "checker boarded" to death in terms of the requirements of wildlife. All too often their

Well-built brush piles can be of great value to various forms of wildlife throughout the year. They especially offer small mammals and birds protection from their natural enemies. Shelters such as this often occur naturally in old growth forests, but unfortunately too many landowners today prefer to "clean" up their woods, thereby removing these important wildlife sanctuaries.

corridors of natural food and cover are literally chopped into pieces. Their movements and shelters are greatly restricted.

Man-made brush piles and even crude rock walls can often provide these animals with travel lanes. As the brush piles deteriorate from year to year, some of the seeds from the animals' droppings will germinate, take root and eventually produce a safe living travel lane.

A good project this winter would be to construct a few brush piles on your property. Ideally you should crisscross five-to-eight-inch-diameter logs (at least six feet or longer) on the bottom two layers. The logs on the very bottom should be spaced four to six inches apart enabling small mammals, such as Cottontails, to find shelter. Use smaller and smaller brush as you crisscross the brush pile and build it upward to around five or six feet high.

You might consider including a few clay drain tiles, at least six inches in diameter, on the ground between the larger logs if you can. These may become very valuable artificial "assists" for the small wildlife, plus it will give them a roof over their heads.

Have you ever been inside a brush pile? I haven't either but hope to before the migratory birds return this coming spring. The idea came from one of Edwin Way Teale's books about nature. He constructed a large, somewhat hollow, brush pile big enough to include a small table and chair. He used it as a photographing blind, a quiet place for writing, and an excellent place for getting close to birds and insects that also used it for their retreat or "hide." The brush in the sides of the pile was spaced loosely enough so that Teale could easily see outward.

In the case that you will have a large quantity of brush resulting from your logging in the woods, or clearing on your property, it is better to construct several small to medium size piles rather than one huge brush pile.

A tall old apple tree, most likely a "sport," grows along the east edge of our garden making the growing of vegetables there difficult as well as alluring to the deer that come for the fallen fruit that is always very sour and wormy. And how the deer used to enjoy our sweet corn before we built a fence around our entire vegetable garden.

A winter activity in the near future will be to transform most of that old tree into several brush piles including one large enough to hold me. My only hope is that they don't become refuges for too many Cottontails who undoubtedly will raise "cane" with our raspberries.

White Paradise

How well we remember helping one of our friends celebrate her birthday several years ago and being treated to an unusual winter sight, sundogs flanking the sun low in the western sky.

The dictionary describes a sundog as a small halo or rainbow near the horizon just off the parhelic circle that, in turn, is defined as a luminous halo visible at the height of the sun and parallel to the horizon, caused by the sun's rays reflecting off atmospheric ice crystals.

In that these lovely short sections of rainbows (sundogs), seen on a cold winter day, are obviously composed of ice or snow crystals, perhaps they more appropriately should be called snowbows (with a long "o").

The *Encyclopedia Brittanica* says that snow is "the solid form of water which grows while floating, rising or falling in the free air of the atmosphere."

The word crystal comes from the Greek word "kryllos" meaning frost. Snow crystals, dainty and brittle, are generally hexagonal in pattern and are grouped by the snow experts into types such as plates, stellars (my favorites), columns, needles, spatial dendrites, capped columns or irregular crystals. They come in a wide range of shapes from simple triangles and hexagons to lacy fern-like dendrites.

I wonder how few people, while enjoying one or another winter spo[rt] give even a passing thought to [a] single snowflake. In reality i[t] is the singl[e] snowflake, multiplied by many billions, upon whic[h] outdoor enthusiast[s] cross-country sk[i,] skate or zi[p] down a hi[ll] on their toboggan.

(Photo by A. Bentley[)]

Snow crystals grow fast whenever there is a rich supply of moisture in the air. It is common for a snowflake to have 50 or more crystals interlocked with each other. No wonder it is said there are no two snowflakes alike.

Even the whispy cirrus clouds five to eight miles high, seen during the summer in the middle to low latitudes, are composed of ice crystals. Cirrus clouds commonly occur at low elevations in the Polar Regions. Remember too that much of the moderate to heavy rains in our area begins as snow.

Having a 1000-foot-long driveway to plow in winter, it is important that I am able to get my plowing tractor started on cold mornings. Hence for many years my tractor was kept in the garage while my car sat outside. Day after day of scraping the frost off the car's windows became somewhat of a stale chore until that magical morning when, concealed beneath a thin layer of snow, just waiting to be appreciated, were hundreds of delicate ice flowers and other dainty white creations formed in their matchless tracery on the inner surface of the glass.

I thank my lucky "snow stars" that one of my sixth grade teachers, Doris Shubert, taught us some of the great literary masters' poems. One of my very favorites was John Greenleaf Whittier's *Snowbound*. I distinctly remember drawing some pictures to illustrate one of my most well-liked passages: "The old familiar sights of ours took marvelous shapes, strange domes and towers rose up where sty or corn-crib stood…"

What a perfect and different world to excite one's imagination, everything in sight coated with white. In that practically all the elementary students (K-8) at the Kewaunee schools walked to school every day it was a rare occasion for school to be called off because of a snow storm.

A "snow day" to us was looked forward to even for the long walk to school. All the exciting overnight transformations along the way were so wonderful to behold. Our vivid "pre-TV" imaginations were greatly heightened as we made our way through the white paradise of billions of snow crystals.

One should be reminded more often to look at the brighter side of life. There really is much hidden value in snow. Many plants are dependent upon an insulating blanket, being an emulsion of air and ice crystals. It melts, feeding the ground water table. In fact snow on high western mountains melts slowly, well into summer, thereby supplying cities and agriculture at lower elevations with precious water.

Consider too its downright beauty and importance to winter recreation, which reminds me – it's time to get the cross-country skis ready for action. Yes, we look forward in more ways than one to banks of snow stars, nature's finest example of six-sided symmetry.

Merlin, The Magician

It's very likely that more people become familiar with birds of prey during the winter than in the summer. Bird-feeding stations outside their homes are eventually bound to attract either a falcon or accipiter, and most birdwatchers who look out at the feeding activity sooner or later witness a predator-prey drama.

The three accipiters (ak-SIP-i-ters) seen quite frequently near people's homes in northeastern Wisconsin during the snowy season are the Northern Goshawk, Cooper's Hawk and the Sharp-shinned Hawk. All have relatively short wide wings, longish tails and are known for their short bursts of speed and agility. They meticulously pluck their victims before tearing into the flesh.

A falcon that we have only occasionally seen during winter months in this region is the American Kestrel. Invariably we observe this jay-size bird perched on a telephone or electric wire as it scans the ditches below for mice.

Buteos (BYOU-tee-os), including Red-tailed and Rough-legged Hawks, the "soaring" hawks, are quite common now as they methodically hunt the open fields for mice, Cottontails and other small mammals. Northern Harriers will also winter this far north. Sporting white rump patches, they can be mistaken for rough-legs that also have similar rump marks. However, harriers generally fly low over the fields, their wings held well above the horizontal, and have a "tippy" flight. Check your field guides and the markings of these birds carefully. You are more likely to be seeing rough-legs than harriers during this season.

A stroke of luck one January in recent years had me sitting on the couch in the study over-looking our bird-feeding area. I was doing some class preparation work and happened to look out the window and notice six Mourning Doves standing in the middle of the cracked corn on the driveway. They were absolutely "frozen" in place which meant only one thing – a hawk, and very near to the doves.

I scanned upward and there it perched on a large Basswood branch about 50 feet from the "petrified" doves. Fortunately my spotting scope was close by and easy to set up quickly in front of the window. The small hawk had obviously killed a Hairy Woodpecker, now in its clutch, just seconds before I looked out the window because it had just started tearing into the victim when I first looked at it through the scope.

Rather heavy brown barring on the breast, tan eyebrows, brown back, barred tail and a very distinct black mark running down its face from the front of its eye were the first field marks I observed. Not a Sharp-shinned, not a Kestrel, too small for a Goshawk - could it possibly be a Merlin, the species that somehow had eluded me all these years?

Within seconds I had *Peterson's Field Guide* opened to the falcon page, indicating very clearly that it was a female Merlin. My respect for Roger Tory Peterson soared as I compared every feature on his painting with the falcon in the Basswood tree.

I hardly budged for at least 15 minutes as I watched this outwardly ravenous hawk gulp down its breakfast. Had the bird in question been an accipiter it would have been plucking its prey. This female Merlin, about 12 inches long, was bolting down everything that it tore off the bird. An entire wing with dangling flesh went "down the hatch," then the tail, head, everything!

As soon as the drama began I assumed that enough of the prey species would be dropped to the snow below enabling me to make positive identification, the thought being that possibly it was a Downy and not a Hairy Woodpecker. I nearly gasped out loud when the first leg was ripped off the woodpecker and, you guessed it, down the entire item went, foot, claws and all. My gosh, what a powerful digestive system that Merlin must have!

Not that I'm bloodthirsty in the slightest (in fact I'm just the opposite). I do regret that I missed seeing the Merlin actually take the woodpecker. One of this hawk's nicknames is the bullet hawk, so blazingly swift is its flight. Ornithologists believe that this may be the only bird capable of catching swallows on the wing, and that's fast. Their prey list is long, including many small bird species along with dragonflies and other large insects in summer, small mammals including bats, and even toads, snakes, lizards, crayfish and scorpions.

Fran Hamerstrom, bird expert whom all Wisconsin birders have respected to the highest degree, says that Merlins are common in Wisconsin only during short periods of spring, fall and during migration, and that indeed they can be found nesting in the northern half of the state. The field guides show that for the most part they winter along the southeastern coast, the Gulf of Mexico and all the way to Peru. Habitually they accompany flocks of shorebirds and other smaller birds during migration ensuring themselves a constant supply of food as they too migrate to warmer climates.

This Sharp-shinned Hawk, smallest of the accipiters in Wisconsin, is an occasional visitor to people's winter bird feeding areas. Invariably it is the weakest, slowest, diseased or physically impaired birds that this swift little raptor takes. One cannot overemphasize the importance of all birds of prey, protected by law in Wisconsin, in helping to maintain a stronger, more fit population of wild birds and mammals.

Its meal completed, now the Merlin fastidiously picked up the leftover bits and pieces and finally wiped its hooked beak several times on the side of the Basswood branch. Several small birds including chickadees and goldfinches came and went from the feeders. The hawk followed their flight with its eyes but remained on its perch for at least another five minutes. Even an unsuspecting Blue Jay came to the platform feeder, snatched a seed and hightailed it into the woods without being chased by the little "bullet."

Something instinctively warned me that any minute the male Red-bellied Woodpecker, our "one and only," would be returning to the feeding area and that's one bird I didn't wish to disappear inside the Merlin's stomach. Binoculars in hand, I cautiously opened the front door and stepped outside.

All the time I slowly approached the little bird of prey, perched at least 30 feet above the ground, it watched my every movement. Finally I was almost directly beneath it before it flew toward the west enabling me to observe it carefully through my binoculars. It headed directly toward the transformer pole south of the garden and with a downward flick of its wings it soared sharply upward and gently alighted on the very top of the pole. What power in its flight! There, typical of the species, it perched while surveying the countryside for its next victim.

How I treasure the total experience, unfortunately at the expense of a Hairy Woodpecker. What a near-perfect way to add a Merlin to a life list of birds. One of my favorite authors on birds, Alexander Sprunt, Jr., wrote in his *North American Birds of Prey*, "It is hard to begrudge this dashing little hawk anything its takes as a natural element of its existence." And so be it!

February

Frigid Feathered Friends

Several years ago we received a phone call from a lady telling of a Mourning Cloak Butterfly flying around her living room. I sensed that she hardly wanted to believe her eyes and what they were seeing. After all, it was February and well below freezing outdoors.

The first question I asked her was, "Do you heat your home with wood?" When she answered in the affirmative, I told her what I thought had happened. The Mourning Cloak – a large dark-brown butterfly with blue dots and a golden yellow band along the margins of the wings – had crawled between the blocks of wood in her woodpile in late autumn and hibernated there. When she brought an armful of firewood into the house she unknowingly also carried in the dormant butterfly.

Yes, there are several butterfly species in Wisconsin that hibernate as adults during the winter and, come spring, emerge to carry on their lives.

What does one do with a butterfly flitting around your house in February? You catch it and gently place it back outdoors in a protected place such as within a woodpile or behind a large piece of bark that has been partly peeled away from a tree.

It is only a periodical crash in the lemming population in the North that forces Snowy Owls farther to the south in search of food. This heavily barred male is about to consume a Green Heron it captured near the shore of Baileys Harbor. The heron had arrived to the area earlier than usual while the owl had lingered several weeks beyond its normal departure date.

It is not uncommon to see, for example, a Comma, Painted Lady, Mourning Cloak or a Milbert's Tortoise-shell Butterfly flying around the woods on a warm sunny day in March with snow still lingering in the shadows. All I can say is that it's quite miraculous that such a creature can withstand sub-zero temperatures for weeks on end, then thaw out and fly away as though nothing had happened.

I've just returned from my thousand-foot walk to the mailbox, glad to be back indoors. I glance at the nearby bird feeders where Evening Grosbeaks, Black-capped Chickadees, Tree Sparrows, White-breasted Nuthatches, Hairy and Downy Woodpeckers and Common Redpolls eat sunflower seeds, cracked corn or beef suet – and it suddenly dawns on me. Those songbirds are being continuously exposed to below-zero temperatures day after day – and surviving! But how? Bear in mind that their food-less nights in early February are between 14 and 15 hours long!

Researchers have found that at 5 degrees F., House Sparrows can live without food for 15 hours, but at 20 degrees below zero F. (25 degrees colder) they can survive only about 10 hours. Obviously they must seek shelter and warmth within a bulky nest that has been constructed inside a barn, stable or other building into which they can gain access. They don't call them House Sparrows for nothing.

At the other end of the scale of hardiness, a Hoary Redpoll that is a more northern nester than its close relative, the Common Redpoll that is widespread in Wisconsin during some winters, is capable of surviving colder temperatures than any other songbird in the Northern Hemisphere. How can they survive while others would perish?

Nature has provided them with small food-storage pouches, called diverticulum (die-ver-TIK-you-lum) in their esophagus, which they fill with high-energy foods, such as Birch seeds, before darkness arrives. Now they are able to gradually digest this food during the night, thereby obtaining the required heat-supplying energy to remain alive.

Snowy Owls surely must experience wind-chill factors of nearly a hundred degrees below zero F. while hunting their prey over the wind-swept expanses of the North Country. Strange as it may seem, the insulation of white birds has been proved to be much better than that of black birds. The same holds true for Arctic Foxes, which in their white winter fur appear to rest comfortably at temperatures of 40 degrees below zero F.

It is commonly known that hummingbirds, such as the Ruby-throated Hummingbird that nests throughout Wisconsin, experience a torpid condition during nighttime hours, their body temperature lowering considerably in order to conserve energy and survive the relatively long food-less period of darkness.

The same thing happens in winter to Black-capped Chickadees, whose body temperature at night is lowered between 10 and 12 percent, resulting in a savings of around 20 percent of their life-supporting energy.

What has also been determined is that the great majority of wintering songbirds in northern latitudes shiver constantly, 24 hours a day. This is an involuntary action, one that they apparently don't even know is occurring, but which enables them to withstand cold temperatures somewhat more easily.

I think of the many Black-capped Chickadees and Red-breasted Nuthatches that we have fed from our hands in winter, and how icy-cold their feet were against our warm fingers on which they perched. Fortunately, the feet and legs of birds are quite wonderful to be able to withstand such extreme cold. Consider ducks and geese that can stand on ice for hours at a time without freezing their feet.

The arteries and veins of their feet are placed directly against each other. The arterial blood flowing to the feet, effecting a rapid replacement of heat loss warms the cold blood returning to the heart via the veins. Observe the ducks long enough and you will see most of them eventually lie directly upon the ice with their feet tucked up into their feathers.

Tree Sparrows from the far north, quite common in this region during most winters, are numbered with many other species that do not spend nighttime hours in cavities for warmth as do birds including woodpeckers, nuthatches and chickadees. Our observations have proved that Tree

Sparrows can survive the cold down to at least 26 degrees below zero F. One researcher examined a dead Tree Sparrow and found that it had 982 seeds in the crop alone.

Our respect for wild songbirds increases every day we watch them successfully survive a prolonged crisis of brutally cold weather. What marvelous creatures they are!

Lady Of The Woods

The tree that impressed me most today during our brisk 10 degree F. hike, that frequently had me looking upward to admire its white beauty against the rich, crystal-clear azure stratosphere, was the Paper Birch. The manner in which this tree's whippy, supple branches and twigs angle so sharply skyward tends to indicate the great flexibility these trees possess.

Look at these conspicuous majestic trees from a distance to see the beautiful red cast their young upper twigs have, a fine contrast with the stark white trunks in late February. I often park near the top of a high hill overlooking a woods and try to identify as many tree species as I can by the color and shape of their winter crowns. The birches are among the easiest.

James Russell Lowell, in his poem, *An Indian Summer*, described the birch as the "most shy and ladylike of trees." Coleridge referred to this immaculate tree as "the lady of the woods." Many people on my tours to observe and study nature were asked if they had any idea why Coleridge called it the lady of the woods. Finally a sharp-minded chemistry professor came up with the best answer of all, "Because the Paper Birch is like a lady, always appealing."

Paper Birches occasionally grow by the thousands on cooler, north-facing, rocky slopes in northeastern Wisconsin where there is lower incidence of the harmful Bronze Birch Borers. One sees more of these beautiful trees while traveling northward on our continent.

To the Ojibwe Indians of our northern lakes region, the Paper Birch was "wigwas." From wigwas came wigwam, because birch bark was often used for covering the top of the small rustic shelter, thereby furnishing it with a waterproof roof. Buckets, baskets, and canoes were fashioned from this splendid material rich in resins and oils. The bark was also used as tinder for starting fires. Miss Emma Toft nicknamed this highly combustible material the "Indians' kerosene." In fact it will work quite well even when wet.

Caress the trunk of a paper birch and your hands will come away with a delightful, chalky, resin-like feel. Indeed its bark, rich with special resins, is extremely waterproof and long lasting. Examine a birch tree that has fallen to the ground some years ago. The wood will be soft and punky but the bark will be in a surprisingly good state of preservation due to the resins and oils. The Native Americans, in their reverence toward this great tree and especially its bark, pointed to the fact that the bark was the last part of the tree to decay.

Roots of the birch were used by some Native Americans as a seasoner in medicines. The sweetish, aromatic, wintergreen-like flavor disguised the less pleasant-tasting doses. Strangely, white people in later years dug and dried the roots of Goldthread plants, having a very astringent, bitter flavor, and added this to many of their patent medicines. The accepted thought of the day was that the more terrible the taste of a medicine, the better it would sell and also cure your ailments.

Our hikes on top of the hard-crusted snow of the early February woods have revealed thousands of birch seeds, along with the very tiny bird-like, cross-shaped "wings" to which the seeds were attached, littering the ground beneath many of the tall stately Paper Birches. On several occasions we caught sight of the birds that had caused this "rain" of seeds to the forest floor, Pine Siskins, Common Redpolls, and American Goldfinches. Birch seeds rank among their favorites. Ruffed Grouse are also known to eat the buds, catkins and seeds of these trees.

The Paper Birch, *Betula* (BET-you-la), the ancient Latin name of a birch, *papyrifera* (pay-pi-RIF-er-a), alluding to its paper-like qualities, is truly a tree of the North. No broad-leaved tree is hardier. In fact it is said to be the only tree native to Greenland and Iceland. They grow to about 66 degrees N. Latitude on this continent. Seven states have many millions growing there, Wisconsin, Minnesota, Michigan, Maine, Connecticut, Vermont and New York. Go to Canada if you wish to see mile after mile of these beauties.

An outstanding example of one of its growth requirements can be seen in hilly regions of its range, especially here at around 45 degrees N. Latitude. Some of the steep northern slopes will contain many birches while relatively few will exist on the southern slopes. One theory presented to me is that the Bronze Birch Borer, a destructive insect to birches, destroying their tips, will not tolerate the cooler shady north slopes but will thrive on the warmer southerly slopes. Birch trees like it cool.

One of the best things that happened during my boyhood was the Sunday afternoon a small group of us, our 7th and 8th grade boys' Sunday school class to be exact, was taught how to swing the birches. Our wonderful teacher, Walter Kacer, knew that an energetic bunch of junior high boys would respond better to his bible teaching if we trusted and respected him. He accomplished this, and extended his teaching as well, by taking us for long hikes in the woods and along the shores near Kewaunee every few weeks after church.

We soon mastered the important art of choosing just the right tree. Size was vital. How we would shinny up the slender trees (which was when I developed a liking for the resin on my hands). Gradually we reached the point where we began to sway slightly to and fro, and then we made the last slow reach upward for that critical and all-important firm grip on the slender trunk.

Now, slow and easy, up came our legs, bent at our hips and knees and braced up against the tree as high as we could bring our feet. Then with a combined kick-off with the feet and outward thrust of the body, holding on for dear life with the hands, we would sail in a slow graceful arc backward, down to the ground. In the case that one particular tree worked unusually well, that tree got ridden over and over until there was no ride left in it. Never, that I can recall, did a birch tree break from our rides.

As Robert Frost so eloquently said in his heartwarming poem, *Birches*, "One could do worse than be a swinger of birches." Yes, I too, like the Native Americans, shall always have deep respect and admiration for "the lady of the woods," always appealing in so many ways!

The Snowflake Man

My world this morning is blanketed with white, feather-light snowflakes. Many individual crystals are falling gently on this wind-free day and remaining intact and unbroken, perfectly but temporarily preserved for studying and enjoying. I shall always refer to this kind of occasion as a "Bentley Snowfall."

The exquisite quieting mood the snowfall produced leads me to thinking, "What would I really like to be doing at this very moment?" I was trained during the early 1950's at the Door-Kewaunee Normal School in Algoma to be a rural school teacher and very fondly recall my practice-teaching days, under the guidance of an excellent teacher, Enid Besserdich, at the little Footbridge School west of Kewaunee.

I think today, in retrospect, back to those days for several reasons. The uncluttered, un-computerized, un-televised, un-hot-lunched, un-hamstrung-by-schedules but nevertheless very challenging school day provided the teacher during the time of the one-room school with incredible freedom to pursue teaching and learning of specific topics at precisely the most opportune times.

Again, in retrospect, here is what I'd be doing with my students today. Every child, from grades one through eight, would own a hand lens. The older children would help the younger children. Each student would have a six-inch piece of black cloth today to drape over one of their coat sleeves and out we'd go, into the great outdoors to study snowflakes and snow crystals.

Oh yes, there's a difference! A snowflake is a "large" cluster of individual crystals. With care, and by using the tip of a feather, you can sometimes separate a single crystal from a snowflake, or, if you're lucky, single crystals will fall onto your dark cloth. You'll quickly learn to exhale slowly and carefully out the side of your mouth to avoid disturbing the tiny, fragile, evanescent objects.

I can easily visualize a dozen or more good "catch hold" points for the children to pursue upon returning to the classroom. Claude Thornhill's recording of "Snowfall" would be playing on the record player and art projects would surely be a high priority.

I'd challenge the students to recreate on paper some of the snow crystal images dancing around in their heads. Have you ever properly folded a piece of white paper, then made intricate cuts with scissors, and finally unfolded it to find a six-sided snow crystal replica? Snow crystals aren't four-sided, they're six or three-sided for the most part. Try it!

Because I love to read aloud, I would schedule some daily reading (and storytelling) from one of my favorite elementary books, *Snowflake Bentley: Man of Science, Man of God,* a biography of Wilson Alwyn Bentley, written by Gloria Stoddard (Concordia Publishing House, St. Louis, 1979). Another beautifully written and illustrated Children's book is *Snowflake Bentley* by Jacqueline Briggs Martin.

Bentley, a bachelor farmer from Jericho, Vermont, a man of small stature but incredibly great accomplishments, became one of the world's authorities on snow crystals Starting at age 19 (1895), he eventually photographed 5,381 snow crystals using a 4x5-inch (negative size) view camera and a microscope that he ingeniously adapted to photographing the delicate, fragile beauty of snow. What a self-taught master of snowflake photomicrography he became!

How well I recall the morning when everything in sight had been liberally and artistically decorated by Jack Frost. The temperature hovered near zero degrees F. and fortunately there was no wind. One after another picture was taken of this dazzling display until fingers and camera refused to function properly.

As Wilson "Snowflake" Bentley put it, a snowflake is "an idea dropped from the sky, a bit of beauty incomparable, that if lost at that moment is lost forever to the world." He didn't dilly-dally during a snowstorm. Other work could wait, but snowflakes couldn't.

Thinking back to my ideal snowflake class, I would have already visited the little town of Jericho, Vermont, lying along Highway 15 about 13 miles east of Burlington, close to the east shore of Lake Champlain. Near the center of the small village, on the Route 15 turn-around, is a marker that reads: "SNOWFLAKE BENTLEY – Jericho's World-famous Snowflake Authority. For 50 years Wilson A. Bentley, a simple farmer, developed his technique of microphotography to reveal to the world the grandeur and mystery of the snowflake, its universal hexagonal shape and its infinite number of lovely designs."

The more easily photographed frost crystals also appealed to Bentley and are what captured my fancy from childhood on. In fact, some of the best formations I've photographed were on the inside of my old van's windshield and on the inside of the woodshed window.

Photography being as advanced and relatively easy as it is today, how challenging it would be for a few students to actually successfully photograph their very own snow or frost crystals. In case you want to see a selection of Bentley's original 4x5 negatives and notebooks some day, they are housed at the Buffalo, New York Museum of Science.

Wouldn't it be fun for some of the children to learn a few of the more than 70 Eskimo words describing snow, where it's fallen, how it's used, where it's encountered, its softness, fineness, hardness and coarseness. A good start would be the *English-Eskimo Dictionary* (Canadian Research Centre for Anthropology, 1970).

How exciting it would be to visualize and express in one's own words the "life" of a snowflake. It begins the instant a nucleus (seed) of volcanic dust or a tiny particle of pollution attracts the very first molecules of water in the upper atmosphere, then moves through varying levels of temperature and humidity, rising and falling often, finally landing on your coat sleeve in snow crystal or snowflake form.

Have you ever heard snowflakes land? The very thought of an entire class of students being absolutely quiet enough so their superb young hearing could actually pick up these sounds is nearly more than a teacher could expect. But it could be done. Here, though, motivated children having individual experiences by themselves at home may produce the best results, as well as the most lasting effects.

In visualizing young children becoming captivated for life by something as outwardly simple and free as a snow crystal, I am reminded of what Bentley's hometown newspaper had to say about this wonderful person following his death: "Longfellow said that genius is infinite painstaking. John Ruskin declared that genius is only a superior power of seeing. Wilson Bentley was a living example of this type of genius. He saw something in the snowflakes which other men failed to see, not because they could not see, but because they had not the patience and the understanding to look.

"Truly, greatness blooms in quiet corners and flourishes under strange circumstances. For Wilson Bentley was a greater man then many a millionaire who lives in luxury of which the 'Snowflake man' never dreamed."

Cold Feet, Warm Heart

When is the last time a Black-capped Chickadee perched on one of your hands? I don't recall the last time but I distinctly remember the first experience during the winter of 1966. Emma Toft had invited me to come to help at the Point that cold December day, and it was on our way along the narrow tree-lined road that we paused to put out table scraps for the animals.

Soon Miss Emma reached into the pocket of her blue denim work coat and pulled out a handful of sunflower seeds. She put a few in one of my bare outstretched hands and told me to stand perfectly still. Much to my amazement a chickadee landed on the tips of my fingers in less than a minute, snatched a seed and flew to a nearby Arborvitae Tree where it immediately began working on its treasured meal.

Mixed with absolute ecstasy was my sudden realization that the bird's feet were icy cold. Then it dawned on me that they couldn't possibly be anything but cold on this near-zero day. Unlike Emma and me whose feet and legs were toasty warm inside insulated boots and trousers, the chickadee's feet and lower legs, as usual, were totally bare.

One can't help but wonder what keeps a small bird like that warm and singing when the temperature drops to well below zero. The fact that Black-capped Chickadees can be found today throughout the Northern Hemisphere, including the Arctic, attests to the fact that they have adapted beautifully through thousands of years to being capable of maintaining their body heat year around.

In the first place the chickadee's high-speed metabolism is a marvel in itself. On a hot summer day with the thermometer reading close to 90 degrees F. a chickadee's heartbeat registers at around 345 per minute, this compared to the average person's 65 to 70 a minute. The lower the outdoor temperature falls the higher the chickadee's heartbeat becomes, for example 674 at 43 degrees F. On a sub-zero day that tiny bird's heart pumps at the phenomenal rate of slightly over 1000 per minute. Should stress suddenly enter the scene, such as a Sharp-shinned Hawk chasing the bird, its heartbeat can jump to somewhat over 1300 a minute.

How well I remember handling my first chickadee during my bird-banding days. I swear that the bird's body was vibrating so fast that I thought for sure its heart was going to jump out of its chest any second. Little did I realize the normal speed of its heart. Surely it too was under stress by my holding it, which further increased its heartbeat.

Not many birds have as thick a coat of feathers per ounce of body weight as does the chickadee. When at rest on a cold day it simply fluffs its feathers outward creating thousands of little pockets of trapped air which, in turn, act as superb insulation against the cold.

A chickadee's legs and feet are little else than bones and tendons which can withstand a great deal of cold. They are not surrounded by fleshy muscles and blood vessels as in mammals. These bones and tendons are put into action by muscles in the bird's warmly insulated thighs.

Some people take one look at the legs of a bird and immediately reach the conclusion that its knees are backward. What they believe are the bird's knees are actually its ankles. Its knees, like a human's, also face forward. However, the bird's knees are snuggled warmly beneath its belly feathers. Yes, a chickadee has proportionately long foot bones!

Check a chickadee's temperature beneath its feathers on a cold day and you'll find that it will be somewhat above 100 degrees F., perhaps around 105. Its feet at the same time will register in the neighborhood of 30 to 40 degrees F.

Chickadees, like nuthatches and woodpeckers, sleep in cavities at night in winter. The warm lining might contain dry grasses, plant down, moss, feathers and even mammal fur. With its legs and feet tucked beneath its body, and its beak also snuggled within its insulating feathers, this small bird can remain remarkably warm during the night.

Even at this season many species of songbirds, including the chickadees, are surviving around 15 hours during the night without food. Assume that the nighttime temperature drops to a minus 20 degrees F., these birds must remain fairly warm in order to survive the night. To say the least, they are marvelous creatures!

Yes, friend chickadee, you warm the cockles of my heart no matter how cold your feet may be!

It is when one examines the service of Black-capped Chickadees in the various ecosystems that several things become very obvious. They have great mobility, varied diets, and considerable differences in habits. They also lay claim to a characteristic of which many people are envious – having extraordinary footloose independence. It must be fun being such a friendly, well-liked happy-go-lucky nomad!

Tacamahac Trees

Today with the temperature above freezing I simply had to go outdoors to stretch my legs and collect some tree and shrub twigs for forcing indoors. February is not complete without several bouquets of fragrant Balsam Poplar and the intricate flowers of Canada Buffaloberry and Moosewood (or Leatherwood) twigs decorating the house. Our very favorite is the Balsam Poplar, better known to old-timers as either Tacamahac or Balm of Gilead.

Ojibwe Indians of this region named this fast growing tree "Manasa'di," the perfume poplar. The large spring buds, stewed in bear fat, yielded an aromatic salve used to cure earaches, to heal wounds, bruises and ulcers, and to soothe boils. The mixture was also rubbed onto the inside of their nostrils so that the balsamic odors could flow through the respiratory passages, opening them in case of congestion from colds and bronchitis.

Several bouquets of the Balsam Poplar twigs scattered throughout our home will soon begin to exude sparkling amber droplets of pitch and will bathe every room with heady balminess. Having slowly absorbed water from the vases, the buds will begin to leaf out in a few weeks. The thin tacky coating of the leaves will intensify the aroma of the twigs.

The Balsam Poplar (*Populus balsamifera*) is widely distributed in the eastern third of Wisconsin and up into the northeastern border of the US. They are by far the largest of the sub-Arctic trees. Early voyageurs plying such rivers as the Mackenzie in the Northwest Territories or the Churchill in Manitoba surely welcomed the sight of these towering trees, as tall as 100 feet, in that otherwise flat and monotonous landscape of the Tundra.

Leaves of the Tacamahac are quite broad, generally oval, pointed at the tip, and have a distinct leathery texture. They are dark olive-green above and light rusty-white below. The bark is smooth and reddish-brown at first, gradually becoming olive-gray and finally brownish-gray and quite deeply furrowed.

The tree can grow 50 feet in 20 years. Unfortunately they are quite prone to canker and develop heart rot. I have seen quite a few Balsam Poplars having been struck by lightning almost as though they are drawn to that awesome atmospheric force.

Look for these trees on the edges of bogs and swamps, riverbanks, shorelines and in bottom-lands as well as along fencelines. Their lives are short and vigorous and they demand plenty of light. Viewed in an ecological perspective they are pioneers like their cousins, the aspens, and serve as nurse trees near the edge of the forest or in openings. Other trees, such as spruces and pines, will grow well in their shade but will eventually overtake and crowd the poplars out of existence.

The poplars of the world can be divided into four groups, the white, balsam, black and trembling. The White Poplar, planted as an ornamental and frequently bordering orchards in this region, is a native of Europe. The Balsam Poplar and the Black Cottonwood (really neither black nor a cottonwood!) represent the balsam group. The Black Cottonwood may be the tallest broad-leaved tree in America, about 225 feet. The well-known and often despised Eastern Cottonwood is a member of the black poplars while the Trembling (or quaking) Aspen and the Large-toothed Aspen belong to the trembling group.

Old-time loggers referred to the Balsam Poplar as "bam," obviously a corruption of Balm of Gilead. Actually the Balm of Gilead (*Populus candicans or gileadensis*) is thought to be a hybrid between the Balsam Poplar and the Eastern Cottonwood. Only pistillate (female) trees exist and can be purchased from some nurseries.

All poplars happen to be dioecious (die-EE-shus), having separate male and female trees. It is the pistillate, or female, trees that one should try to avoid planting as ornamentals. Their long cottony seed catkins, such as on the Eastern Cottonwood, tend to become very messy in spring and will clog eavetroughs and sewer pipes.

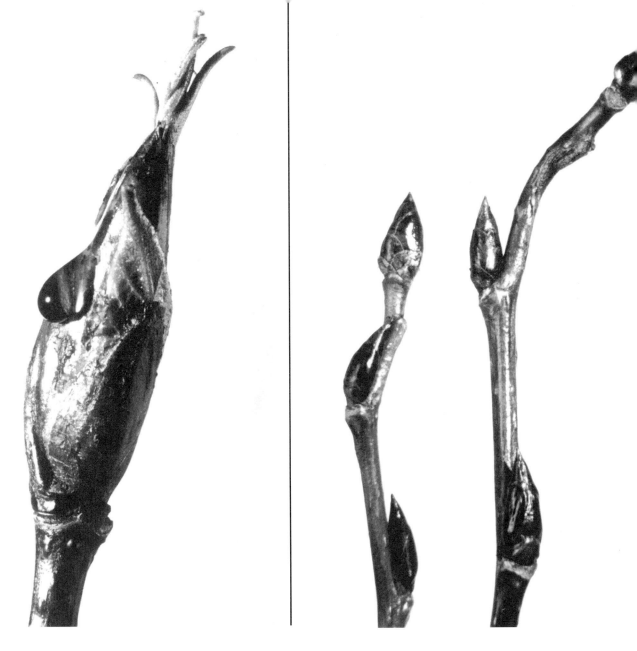

Charlotte and I are grateful to Miss Emma Toft for introducing us to the heady natural perfume of the Balsam Poplar tree. It is the twigs of this fast-growing pioneer species that are cut, placed into vases of water and forced into growth that will add an invigorating breath of spring to your home before the snow carpeting the landscape has melted.

The Lombardy Poplar (*Populus Italica*) is native to Italy and is a variety of the black poplar. They are extremely fast growing, short-lived and dominate the landscape when over-planted as is so often the case. Males generally are taller and more slender while the female trees tend to become quite beamy.

One of the most unusual uses of Tacamahac trees was discovered years ago by beekeepers. It was learned that honeybees collect the fragrant but sticky bud coating, referred to as "bee glue," and use it to seal crevices of their hives or to varnish certain cells in the hive before eggs are laid in them. Consequently many Balsam Poplars or Balm of Gileads were planted near apiaries. Thin veneers of the close-grained wood were used to make berry boxes before the Plastic Age hit us in the midsection.

Early practitioners used the balsam, derived from the enlarged spring buds, for producing cough medicine. The resinous coating was separated from the buds in boiling water. It was listed as having an agreeable, incense-like odor and an unpleasant bitterish taste. Years ago quantities of the balsamic juice were collected in Canada and sent to Europe under the name of Tacamahaca.

My favorite way of experiencing the Tacamahac during all seasons is to firmly squeeze one of the buds between my fingertips, then transfer the sweet-smelling resinous pitch to other parts of my hands. The fragrance lasts and lasts, an entire afternoon if you don't wash your hands!

March

Favorite Stone Fences

It is hard to believe that I just finished plowing six inches of snow this morning and that last week Charlotte and I enjoyed the feel of digging our toes into the soft turf as we walked beside a favorite stone fence. The very thought led me to John Bartlett's *Familiar Quotations*, and it was Henry Van Dyke who said, "The first day of spring is one thing, and the first spring day is another. The difference between them is sometimes as great as a month."

Snow or not, I have pleasant thoughts today, Feb. 24, of a March 28th day a few years ago when I found the first Hepatica wildflowers in full bloom on a sun-drenched south-facing slope in our woods. Wishful thinking!

My thoughts return to our stone fence hike of a week ago today. Like so many stone fences of yesteryear, this one stretches for 40 acres (1320 feet) and is beautifully built. It's easy to admire this magnificent landmark and realize that every stone was fit into place carefully and with thought. I would go so far as to say that this neat farmer, who lived to age 94, was downright artistic in his "laying up of stones." His fences were built to endure and to be practical.

Times and farm machinery have changed whereby it is common practice today to hand pick stones off a field in spring, throw them into the bucket of a front-end loader, and finally dump

How well I remember an experience with one of my students who is one of our county's leading automotive mechanics today. I told him to ask his father if it would be all right for me to look for fossils on one of their stone fences on their farm. Back came a reply the next morning, "Pa sez ya kin have all the fossils ya want, but come and pick 'em when we're pickin' stones in the fields this spring!"

them along a fence line or wherever they will be out of the way. This is by far the most practical, time and labor-conserving method of clearing a field in readiness for spring seeding, and I guess that, were I in farming, I'd do it the same way.

What greatly impressed me in the stone fence we enjoyed again is the interesting variety of erratics stacked so neatly. By erratics I refer to those stones that originated generally many miles to the north of this location and were literally dumped here by one of the glaciers in past years.

Presumably, according to the most scientific evidence provided by modern-day glacial geologists, this area was still beneath several hundred feet of ice eleven thousand years ago. That would be roughly 550 generations ago, figuring 20 years to a generation. When one considers how long ago some of these erratics were formed, then this eleven-thousand-year period is like the wink of an eye on the geological timetable.

The glacial erratic, of all the stones in the fence line, that I have admired many times and always look for, is a bright pink and gray banded beauty. I believe it is genuine Morton Gneiss-schist. Gneiss, pronounced "nice," is a banded or foliated metamorphic rock usually of the same composition as granite, in which the minerals are arranged in layers.

What makes the Morton Gneiss-schist so special is that it is considered to be the oldest dated rock in North America. Some, for example, occurring near the Wisconsin River between Stevens Point and Wisconsin Rapids, has been radiometrically aged at one and ninety-four hundredths billion years old, written 1,094,000,000. I know of two headstones in the Baileys Harbor Cemetery fashioned from Morton Gneiss-schist. This beautiful stone is also called "WESA" stone. Bear in mind that older stones have been found in Greenland and Antarctica.

There are two kinds of black boulders in the long fence that are very eye-catching. One, Gabbro, is dark-colored, coarse-grained, of granitic texture, and contains no quartz. The other is Basalt, black, very fine-grained, heavy, and is often worn and polished to a sheen by many years of glacial "tumbling."

As a college student working for the Kewaunee Highway Department during my summer "vacations," I recall releasing truck-loads of boulders during road construction or repair and marveling at the musical ringing of some of the black boulders as they careened down a slope. Whether or not they were Basalt I don't know, but I distinctly remember calling them "ringers."

Granite-porphyry and plenty of Granite can also be found on the fence. The Granite is usually pinkish, light-colored, coarse-grained and composed of about 30% Quartz and 60% Potash feldspar that may be pinkish-red or black-spotted. The Granite-porphyry resembles Granite but it contains considerably larger crystals of Feldspar, Quartz and Mica.

The large flat pink crystals in some Granite boulders on the fence are of Potassium feldspar. The lovely soft greens in some of the Granites are either Olivine if it is grainy, or Epidote if it is not grainy. The best time to enjoy these colors is during a rain when the stones are wet.

Naturally a lot of the large stones contained within the fence are Dolomite, a darker more dense form of Limestone containing Magnesium. Most of the escarpment in Door County is actually older than the Niagaran Dolomite. In other words it is pre-Niagaran. More properly it should be referred to as Alexandrian Dolomite. The upper part of the escarpment north of Ephraim is Niagaran Dolomite.

Frequently we find holes, called vugs, in the Dolomite resulting from the dolomitization process. If you're lucky you'll find some of these vugs lined with sparkling crystals resembling a geode.

Having explored many stone fences in northeastern Wisconsin I must admit that this is one of the "gneissest" of all!

When you stop to consider that the deciduous trees in our region are leafless for more than half of the year you soon realize how much there is to see and learn from them, how important a part of the October-to-May landscape they really are. Go out at sunset to observe the silhouettes of trees against the western sky. The deciduous species especially seem to display their genuine character best of all at this time of the year.

Tree Silhouettes

Slowly, bit by bit, amber droplet by amber droplet of fragrant sticky sap, the bouquets of Balsam Poplar twigs are coming to life adding wild natural perfume to our home. Within a week or two their light green leaves will be unfurling and it is then that the balmy aroma will have reached its highest peak of perfection. We shall have a two-month jump on the heady spring essence of the great outdoors.

Unless a person is in the woods making firewood for next fall, deciduous trees receive scant attention from most people. They are leafless for around six months of each year, yet their artistic winter anatomy captures hardly a passing glance.

Really it is now that their true beauty and bare bones character, not masked by thick concealing canopies of green foliage, are revealed. Their overall majestic shape, main axis, branching patterns, twigs, buds and other interesting characteristics come to life.

I wouldn't think of walking through a nearby woods without making a special detour to admire two small groves of American Hornbeam, or Blue Beech, trees. Due to the undulating, rippling nature of the trunk of this small, smooth-barked tree it has been nicknamed the "muscle tree." Instinctively I caress a trunk as though shaking hands with Brother Hornbeam and silently wishing it well.

March is a good month for photographing tree silhouettes and to admire the subtle changing colors of some trees' trunks and branches. With stubborn winter slow to give in to fickle spring it is common to have snow plastering the stormward sides of trunks in early morning only to begin melting by noon. The wetted trunks now glisten with totally different colors and appearance until they dry back to their natural conditions.

Give most people an outline drawing of a tree, a box of crayons, tell them to color the tree and invariably the majority will reach for the brown crayon to color the trunk.

Would you like to partake of an interesting exercise? Take a box of crayons, paints or a color chart along on your next hike into the woods and try to match your colors with the tree trunks. Surely there will be dark gray, blackish, whitish-gray, reddish-gray, etc. but seldom brown trunks to match your brown crayon!

Think of the last Red Pine you've seen or perhaps a huge Sycamore tree you've admired on a recent trip southward. Describe in writing the colors and patterns of their trunks. What magnificent objects they are even during their dormancy. My guess is that the druids of ancient history became tree worshippers during the winter months when trees revealed their most beautiful and intriguing individuality.

Another feature about trees that most people don't think about is that they are flowering plants. Granted their exquisitely tiny flowers don't resemble tulips or roses, but nevertheless each species of tree flower has its own singular shape and beauty.

A classic book to help in your study and appreciation of this seldom noticed annual phenomenon is *Tree Flowers of Forest, Park and Street* by Walter E. Rogers. He was for many years a professor of botany at Lawrence College, Appleton. His greatly enlarged photographs are spectacular as are the numerous small drawings and winter silhouettes done by Olga A. Smith, then an instructor in botany at Lawrence College (now Lawrence University). The book has been reprinted by Dover Publications, Inc.

One can go on and on listing the attributes of trees including that of providing us with shelter, beautification of property, wildlife food and habitat, shade and distinctiveness for our streets and highways, and life and character to our landscape.

In addition to the thousands of products of the forest contributing to our day-by-day life, so do living trees bring beauty, relaxation and enjoyment into our lives during all seasons of the year.

Many people, including myself, look at trees as the oldest, largest and most massive living things on our planet. Take the Bristlecone Pine for example. These gnarled, stunted, deformed trees growing in harsh dry climates at high elevations in some western states began their growth before the building of the Great Pyramids in Egypt.

Do you suppose these same magnificent old monarchs may still be alive when true harmony and total peace will prevail among people and with nature throughout the world?

I'm Taking A Lichen To You

Invariably there comes a time in March when the outdoor temperature remains above freezing for several consecutive days. However the woods are still "bare bones" and it'll be a while before the flowering plants come into bloom.

One group of native plants can be at its yearly best during these welcome mild breaks in the weather. There are few waterless spells to discolor and dry them out, and the readily available moisture can make the intricate beauty of these seldom-noticed plants reach their very best. I speak of the lichens.

It doesn't surprise me one bit that the majority of people couldn't care less about these miniature, inconspicuous plants. Unfortunately they don't produce colorful blossoms and, to make matters worse, few have even been given common names.

Who in their right mind would get carried away with *Trypethelium virens* or *Verrucaria nigrescens*? How does one pronounce them in the first place? Many little kids all over the world can easily rattle off the long, cumbersome scientific names of a dozen or more dinosaurs or other prehistoric animals, but there's excitement attached to dinosaurs. The scientific names of lichens and most other plants sadly go begging.

Strong winds this past week did some natural pruning in our woods, and during my daily walk to the mailbox I came across a Basswood branch lying on the driveway loaded with beautiful lichens. Soon I was seated at my desk, peering through a hand lens at the interesting shapes and colors of the crusty, gray-green lichens.

At first I thought the specimen was in the genus *Parmelia* (par-MEE-lee-a), one of the lichens used by the Ruby-throated Hummingbirds in the construction of their nests. After examination, followed with poring through some references, I decided it was an *Anaptychia* (an-ap-TYKE-ee-a) lichen. It was prominently margined and contained fascinating blackish discs.

Each roundish "fruiting" disc is called an apothecium (a-po-THEE-see-um) – plural would be apothecia – and it contains spores that are vital to the reproduction of the plant. Lichens, mushrooms, mosses, ferns, clubmosses and horsetails are among those plants that can reproduce from spores, as opposed to garden vegetables and flowers, for example, that reproduce from seeds.

There are two well-known and admired lichens of this region that can grow to a half-inch or even taller and whose fruiting bodies have led to their names. One, the British Red Soldier lichen, *Cladonia cristatella* (cla-DOE-nee-a cris-ta-TEL-la), has gray-green "stems" topped off with red-tipped fruiting bodies. It often grows on rotting wood.

The other familiar relative in the same *Cladonia* genus is the Pixie Cup lichen, whose appearance reminds me of the shape of a golf tee. The tiny cups act as splash cups. Raindrops fall into them and are rebounded outward and away from the plants, at the same time carrying with them the spores that are dispersed away from the parent plant.

There's another lichen of this region which quite a few hikers know, the Reindeer Moss. Here is a plant that grows upright like a moss so, unfortunately, it is commonly called a moss when in

It is along a road hugging the shore north of Baileys Harbor that several trees are royally decorated with long healthy growths of a species of Old Man's Beard lichen. Northern Parula Warblers use these dense hanging clusters of grayish green lichens in which to construct their nests. Pollute their air, which in turn will kill these ultra-sensitive lichens, and one does away with the nesting warblers as well.

reality it is a lichen. Reindeer lichens during humid days can be as soft and comfortable to the touch as a wet kitchen sponge.

The scientific name of the Reindeer "Moss" is *Cladina rangiferina* (cla-DIE-na range-if-er-EYE-na) and it is gray-green in color. Reindeer of the North prefer to eat a related yellowish species, *Cladina mitis* (MY-tis), due to its milder taste. *Mita* refers to being mild since this species contains less usnic acid than other related species.

There are roughly 37,000 species of lichens in the world. Wisconsin is home to about 600 species, while one could find about 2,000 species in the Arctic. Your search for lichens in large industrial cities will usually end in failure. Even though lichens adapt by making use of small amounts of moisture and can make their food in a hurry, they are extremely intolerant of polluted air.

As an example of the large number of lichens one can expect to find growing in a pristine natural area, lichenologists have recorded around 130 species of so-called macrolichens at Toft Point, an old-growth forest near Baileys Harbor, Wisconsin. This number does not include quite a few of the so-called crustose lichens, some which appear as little more than thin black dirt on rocks or as whitish dusty material on Northern White Cedar trees.

Earlier in this story I mentioned a lichen, *Verrucaria nigrescens* (ver-ru-CARE-ee-a ni-GRES-sens). This fussy plant grows as a thin blackish layer only on limestone and therefore literally abounds in northeastern Wisconsin. Its species name, *nigrescens,* refers to its black appearance.

The other lichen I listed was *Trypethelium virens* (try-pe-THEE-lee-um VERE-ens). These blotchy, dark, crusty, grayish-purple lichens grow only on American Beech trees, making these interesting little plants quite easy to locate, there being so many of these large, gray, smooth-barked trees in eastern Wisconsin.

I view lichens as coal miners of years ago would have depended upon their caged canaries which, by simply remaining alive and alert, signaled to the underground workers that the air was "safe" to breathe.

One of my most favorite of all lichens in this part of the state is the Old Man's Beard lichen, a member of the *Usnea* (UZ-nee-a) genus. Don't confuse the Old Man's Beard lichen with the Spanish Moss plants that grow in their lacy, draped forms on so many trees in the South. Even though these lovely plants look like moss, they are actually flowering plants belonging to the pineapple family! What pleases me is that the species name of the Spanish Moss is *usneoides* (uz-nee-OY-dees) because of its close resemblance to the Old Man's Beard lichen.

Usnea lichens, of which there are about 600 species in the world and whose identity depends largely upon their intricate branching patterns, are virtually extinct today in all of Europe due to the extremely high degree of air pollution there. I dread the day when these lichens disappear from this region of northeastern Wisconsin because not only will it reflect a poorer quality of air, but a favorite warbler, the Parula Warbler, builds its nest in hanging clusters of these fussy plants. When the *Usnea* lichens disappear from the region, so will the Parula Warblers.

Even though silent and very small, the lichens could very well be saying: "This clean, healthful air appeals to us. We like it here!"

I have great respect for the person who understands and appreciates the American Crow. It has occurred to other people in various places throughout history that, if animals were classified according to what they do rather than by physical characteristics, crows would be the most closely related to humans. This American Crow was photographed on a sub-zero day and displays frost around its eyes and on its beak.

In Defense Of Crows

During the 39 years I spent in a classroom, 19 as a student and 20 as a teacher, there was no species of bird more than an American Crow, with its raucous mocking voice, that reminded me of my "imprisonment" and made me yearn to be outdoors each spring enjoying my freedom instead of being cooped up in a building.

I can even imagine whining and complaining as a junior high student to my parents, "How do the teachers at school expect a guy to study while the windows are wide open, sweet fresh air is flowing into the classroom, and outdoors the crows are flying by, cawing, free as the breeze?" It's not difficult to imagine my Dad replying, "Do you suppose the crows are smarter than you?"

While I refuse to offer an answer to the hypothetical question asked of me by my Dad, it was the Rev. Henry Ward Beecher who issued an interesting and frequently-quoted statement many years ago: "If men (people!) had wings and bore black feathers, few of them would be clever enough to be crows."

I recall reading that the brain of a crow is larger in proportion to its body size than any other species of bird and, supposing that life on our planet ceased to exist in order of its intelligence, ability to find food and water, etc., the last relatively large creature to survive would be the crow.

One thing I do know is that crows, like the majority of people, have become urbanized. Friends living on the outskirts of a large metropolitan area tell of huge crow roosts of thousands of birds that are causing the citizens untold misery. Surely this success story can be attributed directly to the intelligence and adaptability of these omnivorous, highly social and communicative birds. An estimated population of about 3 billion of these amazingly hardy creatures in North America today clearly tells me that they like it here!

Don't go into the deep woods in search of crow nests. In fact they prefer a combination of small woodlots and broad cultivated fields. Golf courses are OK too! The layout of most cities and suburbs complete with open glades and groves of evergreens is ideal for their nesting and finding food. Along with Red-winged Blackbirds, European Starlings and Common Grackles, the crows are extremely capable of living with people, and of surviving well in spite of them.

The widely-used mechanical harvesting implements in today's agriculture were made to order for the survival and easy food-finding of crows — and blackbirds, starlings, grackles and cowbirds as well. My friend, Carl Scholz, said that a crow is as much a part of a farm as is a barn. The next logical question might be, "Do all these crows ever benefit people?"

Naturally there has been research done to get to know more about these crafty birds. One estimate is that a single crow family kills and consumes about 40,000 or more harmful insects including grasshoppers, beetles, moths, caterpillars, wire worms, grubs, army worms etc. during the nesting season alone, food that is unusually high in protein. The young crows are in the nest for five weeks and, during that period eat half their own body weight in food daily!

Knowing that our friends, the Scholz's, have had pet crows at THE Farm in past years, I asked Carl what it was like to have a crow around the house. His reply was that a crow is the finest pet in the world. In fact he said that their family often had crow for breakfast, that is, as a "guest," not to eat! It would sit on the back of a chair (where it usually wasn't appreciated, especially by the four children) and beg for food.

Its most favorite food was scrambled eggs, rich in protein. Carl, having had a lot of experience caring for and feeding baby chicks, realized that young birds require a high protein diet, and that as soon as they don't receive enough of this important substance their wings begin to droop and the birds becomes listless.

This factor could very well account for crows' occasional appetite for wild bird eggs, as well as chicken eggs, while they are nesting. Being early nesters in general, it sometimes becomes difficult for them to locate, for example, large insects to feed to the young. Cold wet springs can be devastating on many insect populations. Carl has seen them locate a clutch of chicken eggs, drive their bills into an egg and carry it back to the nest. In the case you are wondering — no, I do not condemn crows for doing what comes naturally and what they most likely have been doing for eons, any more than I would criticize you for having a cow killed so you could have roast beef for dinner tonight!

One challenge our friends have had with their pet crows was "Blacky's" strong attraction to shiny objects such as necklaces, fountain pens, coins, and even clothespins. Woe be unto the lady wearing shiny earrings, and on whose shoulder the crow was harmlessly perched. Ouch! Ernest Thompson Seton's famous yarn, "Silverspot, the Story of a Crow," contained in his book, *Wild Animals I Have Known*, also dwells on Silverspot having been a notorious collector of "valuable" glistening things.

Fortunately I am not continually confined to a building during my "retirement" and can be outdoors at my leisure watching, admiring and listening to the music of the crows. Luckily their singing is low-pitched, well within my hearing range. However, this is not what prompted me to write about crows today. For the first time ever, licensed gunners can legally shoot crows in our state for a period of 124 days. The split season runs generally from early February through March 20, then continues from September 15 through November 21. Apparently those who approved the season and established the dates realized that crows do have value in nature and that they should be given protection from the shooters during nesting season.

One gripe I have is that a lot of hunters, in my opinion, would have difficulty distinguishing an American Crow from a Northern Raven. Unfortunately crows don't always say "caw caw," and both the raven and crow are large black birds. What will crow hunters do with the dead birds? Beats me! Could hunting crows be little else than an excuse to legally be shooting at something alive during especially the February-March period when they shouldn't be banging away in the woods in the first place?

What a thrill it is to know that, fragile as they may be, some species of butterflies are capable of spending a sub-zero Wisconsin winter in the adult stage. Included in this hardy group is this Anglewing, the Comma Butterfly, photographed as it absorbed the warmth of the early spring sun while sitting on our front sidewalk. Notice the white "comma" mark on its underwing surface.

There was a time when gunners considered there to be an unending supply of Passenger Pigeons and literally slaughtered millions upon millions of them. Extinction is a very final thing! All of the Passenger Pigeons are gone – forever! My hope is that the crows won't be next!

Frail Children Of The Air

We recently received a lovely "troll" postcard from one of our friends, Ingrid Jonsson, who was traveling in Sweden. What immediately caught our eye was the beautiful colored butterfly stamp featuring what to the Swedes is the "Sorgmantel. "

In small print below the butterfly is its scientific name, *Nymphalic antropa*, the so-called international name used by scientists in all countries where this large butterfly lives. We in the United States call it the Mourning Cloak butterfly.

The wings and bodies of these three-inch-wide creatures are deep purplish-brown, velvety and, in fact, quite hairy. Even the surfaces of their eyes are covered by fine hairs. A broad yellow band on the outer margins of their wings is highlighted by a row of light blue spots as seen from above, just inside the band. Two white spots adorn the outer edge of each forewing.

Describe this butterfly to someone from England and the response may be, "Oh, do you mean the Camberwell Beauty?" The first Mourning Cloak butterflies caught in England were thought to have traveled there as adults on barges carrying wooden posts from Finland. They were captured in 1748 in the rustic country village of Camberwell on the outskirts of London and called the Camberwell Beauty. Today Camberwell has lost its country charm and instead is a bustling metropolitan borough of London containing more than 250,000 people.

The Mourning Cloak was the last butterfly we saw on our property last year, on a sunny November day. What continually amazes us is that this very butterfly is in all likelihood spending the winter, as an adult, inside a woodpile, brushpile or behind a large flap of loose bark on a dead tree.

I wish I could explain the chemical change that occurs in this butterfly's body fluid, preventing the water cells from freezing and bursting. Could this life-preserving chemical be something like the ethylene glycol which, when added to the water in your car's radiator, prevents it from freezing?

Many other insects, including cluster flies and several other species of butterflies, can withstand below-freezing temperatures. In some years the first adult butterfly I see, usually in March at our home in the woods, is Milbert's Tortoise-shell, a small, predominantly black, orange and white butterfly that has over-wintered as an adult. Anglewings, such as the Comma, are also spending the winter in diapause, their period of inactivity.

All butterflies of this temperate region spend the winter in diapause. Depending upon the species, this long cold period of inactivity may be in any one of the four life states: egg, larva, pupa or adult.

The tiny Hairstreak butterflies over-winter in the egg stage. Two of our favorites, the White Admiral and the Viceroy, spend the winter in the larva, or caterpillar, stage. Depending upon the latitude, a Red Admiral may over-winter in either the pupa or adult stage.

The only highly regular migratory butterfly from this part of the world is the Monarch. It is only the last generation of at least three during each summer in this area that has the instinct to migrate. Monarchs that leave northeastern Wisconsin head southward between late August and throughout September ending up in the high, fir-clad mountainous region west of Mexico City.

Let's say these migratory Monarchs emerged from their chrysalises some time in early September, migrated and, after wintering in a rather dormant condition at slightly above 50 degrees F. in Mexico, headed northward in early spring. These butterflies mated and died around six to eight months after their lives as adults had begun last September. The eggs laid by the female before dying hatched and those offspring found their way to our state by late May and into early June.

A scholarly lepidopterist (one who studies moths and butterflies) of years ago described them as "frail children of the air." Surely the Mourning Cloak and several others would rear up on their wings, could they communicate verbally with us, and voice disagreement with this depiction.

We bask indoors in our warm home on this cold, windy, March day wondering where the November Mourning Cloak butterfly is at this moment. Hopefully on our walk out to the mailbox on a calm, sunny day before the month is over this wonderful insect will nonchalantly sail above our heads, and we will be more awed and respectful than ever of this hardy but frail partner in nature.

April

The Sweet Sugar Maple

A tree that is native to northeastern America, and nowhere else, reigns supreme as the world's overall most beautiful broad-leaved tree. Drip some pure maple syrup onto your pancakes or waffles and you will have tasted one of the finest and most healthful forms of sweetening known to man. We Wisconsinites, along with folks from Vermont and New York, can be proud that the Sugar Maple has been chosen as our state tree.

This outstanding species is without a doubt the best known and most important maple in the United States, if not the entire world, today. We can thank the Native Americans for discovering the general process of evaporating the sap to obtain the sweetened syrup and sugar. Over 10 million Sugar Maples are tapped each spring, the most being in Vermont.

The tree's hard, smooth-grained wood weighs about 44 pounds per cubic foot and is renowned for its use in fine furniture, floors and musical instruments. Certain parts of high quality pianos are made of this prized wood. Some of you may have a wooden rolling pin made of maple. My Mother gave me a large maple cutting board, in the shape of a pig, made and given to her by her Uncle Frank Cmejla (SHMAY-la, a Czechoslovakian name) for a wedding present in 1926. We use it daily and it's as good as new.

As much as we look forward to the flowering and leafing out of trees, we also admire their distinctive character as revealed in their bare winter silhouettes. One of our favorites is an open-grown tree that consequently has a broader form as well as lower branching. Its trunk is relatively short compared to the tall telephone-pole-like trunks of forest-grown maples. There a maple can attain the height of 35 feet in 20 years.

Moist well-drained slopes are their best environments where they do well with American Beech, Paper Birch and Eastern Hemlock. They will not tolerate wet, acid soils. Prime growing conditions can result in a 120-foot-tall tree having a diameter of five feet. The largest specimen I have located and measured in Door County (at Whitefish Dunes State Park) is slightly over 12 feet in circumference with a diameter of about three feet ten inches, measured at 4 1/2 feet above the ground.

Deer are very fond of young maple saplings and eat large quantities of them in winter. As a result, more and more maple-beech-hemlock woods are slowly reverting to predominately beech woods. As long as the deer population remains high the total number of maples, as well as hemlocks, will gradually diminish until the day in future years when they will be quite rare here. Deer do not eat small beech trees, only the nuts of mature trees, but they love maple and hemlock.

A lot of people will look up at the first hint of green on the maple trees in spring and think they are seeing the emerging leaves when in reality they are viewing the tiny inconspicuous greenish-yellow flowers. They're said to be perfect flowers in that both stamens and pistils (male and female) are produced on each flower. Certain trees, such as ashes, willows and aspens have male flowers on one tree and female on another. They are said to be dioecious (die-EE-shus) trees.

Come fall and winter, a maple tree that has lost its leaves is quite obviously not dead. It is dormant but very much alive. Call them economical if you wish, for about 90% of the minerals in their leaves by autumn is transported downward and stored in the tree's lower tissue. With the warmth of spring, enzymes within the tree are stimulated into action. The tree's stored starch begins to change into sugar which, through a laborious and time-consuming series of events, may end up on your flapjacks in the form of syrup.

Once the leaf and flower buds, formed during the past summer, begin to expand with fluids and unfold, then the pressure within the tree trunk, required to cause the delicately-sweetened sap to drip, no longer exists. Now an intricate relationship between electrical charges and molecules of water, coupled with the marvelous osmotic pumps and cellular cross-walls, enables this life-giving fluid to reach a tree's highest leaf. For the tallest tree in the United States, such as a Coastal Redwood, this may be higher than a football field is in length, over 300 feet.

What a miracle of leaf production these maples will produce. As soon as the new leaves are fully developed by early June the vital on-going summer work of the trees begins, including manufacturing winter buds. These marvels of packaging, waterproofed protective coats to guard them from drying out, and winterized to prevent them from freezing, are completed by the start of September. Now a substance called dormin will check their winter growth. They will be inactivated for about seven months.

A large Sugar Maple tree develops as many as two million buds. Approximately one-half of them will open the following summer while the unopened exist as a living insurance to the tree. In case leaves or even large branches may be blown off during a storm, the nearest undeveloped buds open to take the place of those leaves destroyed.

The buds on maples are produced in threes at the end of each twig. The tallest one is in the center, flanked by two shorter ones. All winter long the buds have been protected from the elements by bud scales. Come spring, most of these protective bud scales will fall off, thereby leaving distinctive bud scale scars encircling the twig. Close examination will reveal a number of series of these rings on each twig. The interval between each set of scale scars indicates one year's growth. The intervals on lower or inner twigs are usually considerably shorter than those on upper or outer portions of a tree.

April is when "sweet water" is collected from Sugar Maple trees in this region, leading to the production of one of the most ambrosial foods imaginable. Find yourself an imposing Sugar Maple — even though you may not own it — watch its subtle changes from day to day, season to season, and let it be your spring parade marshal, steadfast and strong yet delicate and delicious, king of all the broad-leaved trees.

Surely the Sugar Maples have taken over as the number one street-side tree in the United States due to the large and unfortunate die-off of millions of American Elms. Perhaps the maples tend to be more of a small town tree than a large city tree being very sensitive to the air pollution produced by heavy traffic and industry.

Regardless of where you live in this area, locate an imposing Sugar Maple, watch its developments from day to day, and let it be your spring parade marshal, steadfast and strong yet delicate and delicious, king of all the broad-leaves.

Chippie

It was seven years ago that I first had the pleasure of gently scratching the back of a young chipmunk. One of the young Eastern Chipmunks in the yard, about three-fourths grown, had become unusually tame and would come out immediately to get some cracked corn as I scattered it onto the ground.

Talking to it in soft, gentle tones I slowly reached downward with hand extended. To my surprise it continued to feed, ignoring me completely. Finally I began scratching the top of its rump, and to my amazement it never budged. Apparently that little squirt hadn't learned a thing from its parents about the extreme dangers of *Homo sapiens*, number-one enemy of most wildlife.

As a rule we don't make special efforts to become friendly with wildlife that comes to our feeders. We have on occasion lured Black-capped Chickadees and Red-breasted Nuthatches to our outstretched hands and a treat of sunflower seeds, but that's about all.

Several weeks ago I happened to be scattering cracked corn near the edge of the driveway, the same place where I have been doing this for the past twelve years. Suddenly out from the underbrush scooted a chipmunk and proceeded to "vacuum" up the bits of cracked corn as fast as I tossed it down, practically under my feet.

Slowly I kneeled down and reached toward the tiny mammal and, much to my surprise, it totally disregarded my presence as it continued gathering its corn. Now I ever so slowly began scratching its back and, again, the tame creature hardly budged. In fact I swear that, after several seconds of scratching one of its flanks, it turned slightly as though to say, "Would you please scratch this side for a while!" I seriously doubt that this is the same animal that confided in me seven years ago. For all I know it may be one of its offspring genetically programmed to trust people!

Four different chipmunks vie for the daily handout of cracked corn and especially sunflower seeds scattered upon the ground. Each has its own den in different directions. My tame friend scampers to the large brush pile south of the garage, a distance of around 75 feet from the feeding area.

Naturally I have become quite fond of this little squirt and find great enjoyment in being brought down to its level. What a great way to begin the morning, by putting out a little food for the wildlife, kneeling down, talking softly to the animal, scratching the back of one of your favorite little partners in nature, and finally giving thanks for another day.

A few years ago my friend, Mike Madden, and I spent several days camping and exploring on Drummond Island located near the west end of Lake Huron, southeast of Sault St. Marie. A number of times we observed what we were sure were Least Chipmunks, considerably smaller than the so-called Eastern Chipmunks with which we are so familiar in Door County.

In general they are more active and noisy than the Eastern Chipmunks. Golly, those tiny mammals could really move! Zoologists tell us that there are four distinct sub-species of chip-

Even though chipmunks may appear very similar, they possess very different appearances and characteristics. The one that races onto our deck most summer mornings appears to be looking for me, wondering when I will be out to present it with its daily offering of sunflower seeds. It is quite dull-colored but so tame that it allows me to scratch its back as it feeds from my hand. Others are much brighter in their coloring and also very shy, running to hide before I come within five or six feet of them.

munks in Wisconsin. The Gray Eastern Chipmunk (the "big" one) occupies the northern two-thirds of the state and generally is around 9 and a half to 11 inches long including the tail.

The Ohio Chipmunk, slightly smaller, duller and more brownish is found in the southern third of the state. Quite restricted to Door County, northeastern Brown County, Kewaunee and perhaps Manitowoc Counties is the Peninsula Chipmunk. It too is slightly smaller than the Eastern Gray and also paler and more coppery in color.

The smallest variety is the Least Chipmunk found in Oconto, Marinette and western and northern counties along with the larger Gray Eastern. The Least is about 7 and one-half to 8 and one-half inches in total length and has more distinct facial markings than the others. I suspect, but cannot prove, that hybrids between sub-species do occur.

Fruits, nuts, seeds, insects and cultivated grains make up most of the chipmunks' diet. However, friends of mine who grew many bulb flowers such as lilies, tulips, hyacinths and daffodils had a considerable number of the bulbs dug up and eaten by those impetuous little critters.

Not having the heart to kill them, they bought several live-traps and baited them with peanuts in the shell. Apparently those delicacies were pure ambrosia to the chipmunks. In fact they didn't appear to be too concerned over being captured and, while in the trap, proceeded to cram as many peanuts, shells and all, into their generous-sized cheek pouches.

How grotesque those flippant little scamps were, their heads appearing to be twice their normal size! By the end of summer my friends had trapped and taken away from their five acres more than 75 saucy, well-fed chipmunks. You might suspect that about as fast as my friends removed chipmunks from their property others from neighboring woods moved in to take the place of those departed. It has been said that nature abhors a vacuum!

People often confuse the Eastern Chipmunk with the Thirteen-lined Ground Squirrel, also erroneously called the gopher. "Chippies" are about 10 or 11 inches long, two-fifths of that being tail. They have two light stripes and three dark stripes on the sides of their face. Five dark stripes and four light brown or gray ones extend down their back to a rust-colored rump. Underparts are a light cream or fawn color.

Even though we don't see them in most years from early November to the beginning of April, experts tell us that these solitary animals are not true hibernators. They will be awake in their dens on many winter days. Their food cache, containing dried cherries, blueberries, gooseberries, acorns, beech nuts, maple seeds, sunflower seeds, wheat, corn or oats, is very near to them. In fact they may be sleeping on top of it.

How we treasure the trusting companionship of chipmunks, partners in nature that frequently bring us down to our knees.

Thoreau And Earth Day

This is being written a few days before Earth Day, April 22, with the question in mind, "Shouldn't every day be Earth Day?" Why can't every man, woman and child be led to do something every day of their lives that would increase their respect for Mother Earth, enrich their sense of wonder and love toward all life, and inspire them to do everything in their power to help heal Earth's deepening wounds.

Some unexplainable spirit tugs at me, lures me into the primeval old-growth pine forest that stands virtually untouched by human hands. As the Native Americans lived respectfully in or close to this awesome wooded area, I too can hike the primitive trails among the towering trees and inhale the invigorating evergreen-scented air. A half-mile into the deep woods one is magically removed from the on-going racket of society.

Time after time I have walked into the depths of this magnificent "cathedral," not built by human hands, without meeting a person or even evidence of a human being. Henry David Thoreau said, "I should be pleased to meet man in the woods. I wish he were to be encountered like wild caribou and moose."

In reading through my copy of Thoreau's Journal, 1837-1861, one learns that he studied nature because he felt that this was a vital part of every person's background, essential to a good life. It was his belief that people can derive great strength from daily contact with the earth and with nature.

Thoreau hoped during his lifetime that certain lands would remain undeveloped, preserved for the public, "if only to suggest that earth has higher uses than we put her to."

He went on to say, "If a man walks in the woods for love of them half of each day, he is in danger of being regarded as a loafer; but if he spends his whole days as a speculator, shearing off those woods and making earth bald before her time, he is esteemed an industrious and enterprising citizen."

I pick up my pace as I head for the "Little Bayou" that gently dents the eastern rocky shore of this inspiring White Pine forest. Common Goldeneye Ducks and Red-breasted Mergansers engage in their splashing and neck-stretching courtship a hundred yards offshore, and a lone motorboat with two sport-fishermen, trolling slowly toward the open water, produces the only faint man-made sound of the morning heard in the woods during my outing.

The east wind carries my scent into the forest as I hike, and consequently I hear the deer moving away from me before I see them. What sounds like a love-sick American Crow caws over and over from the top of a tall White Spruce, the big black bird not stopping or even hesitating when I walk directly below. It too must feel very secure as I do in this pocket of several hundred acres of wilderness.

My thoughts drift to a recent television documentary telling of the potentially dangerous situation looming in the Netherlands where the flower and flower bulb growers have pumped so many gallons of chemical fertilizers, herbicides and insecticides into the ground through the years seriously threatening the drinking water of a huge region, perhaps for many years to come. I think to myself, "How unbelievable, for the clean, tidy, spotless Dutch to continue to do something as horrible as this!"

My next question, not only aimed at the tulip bulb growers but all of us directly or indirectly responsible for the deplorable condition of our earth, its air included, is, "Who will be responsible for cleaning it up?" Will the present-day industrialists and agriculturists and orchardists, plus all drivers of cars, etc. insure the following generation that the soil and water and air will be clean and pure when they inherit it?

I strongly suspect that the opposite will be true, that the young folks all the way down to the toddlers of today will have to shoulder an unbelievable burden in years to come, cleaning up the mess in order that sufficient jobs be made available for people to live the lifestyles that have evolved to the present in which so many millions of humans obviously appear to be irreversibly locked.

Ironically so many of these young people are being taught and led to believe that to not litter and to recycle are next to godliness. Both are important yet are such an infinitesimal part of repairing our gasping earth. We pick litter along our neighborhood roadsides too, and seriously work at recycling, but shake our heads in bewilderment and helplessness when confronted with the steadily deteriorating conditions of our Mother Earth and Father Sky.

I have seen some mighty good environmental education going on in our schools recently and wonder if this is our greatest hope for salvation. From what we have observed and heard from both political parties in past years of election campaigning, we find ourselves terribly dejected and crestfallen. There is little light at the end of the dark tunnel leading toward a cleaner, safer environment in which to live.

How incredibly wonderful it would be if every day could be celebrated as Earth Day. Good stewardship of our Mother Earth and Father Sky, still quite rich with natural resources, would become a common practice with every man, woman and child. Beautiful rural vistas would be included among other ecologically valuable areas to be carefully managed and preserved.

Drum And Bugle Corps

A few days ago Charlotte and I, along with the members in our early-morning birdwatching class, were turning into our driveway when there, poised like a lifeless statue, stood a Ruffed Grouse within 20 feet of the van. Immediately I turned off the engine and all of us, binoculars trained on the chicken-like bird, carefully glassed the stealthy creature.

Having had the pleasure of similar experiences in the past, we called our friends' attention to the tip of the bird's tail. One could quite clearly see that, even though the tail feathers were drawn together, the top-most ones lacked the dark half-inch-wide band. Had her tail been fanned out-ward, the black band would have been interrupted by two or three lighter central feathers. Usu-ally, but not always, the male's fanned tail shows a continuous unbroken black band near the edge.

As soon as I started the car and began moving forward toward the grouse she put down her head and ran into the underbrush to hide. Ruffed Grouse, typical of other gallinacious birds, often apparently find more safety by running than by flying.

Two of my most favorite of all wild bird songs could be heard as I worked in the garden yesterday. A Sandhill Crane bugled repeatedly from our neighbor's field to the west while a cock Ruffed Grouse drummed every few minutes from his favorite drumming log around 100 yards southeast of our house. I strongly suspect, and hope, that this grouse has mated with the hen grouse we saw a few days earlier on the nearby driveway.

Even though we have to be downright lucky to be able to lead our friends to a live grouse, we can at least show them the bird's droppings decorating his half-rotten, moss-covered drum-ming log. I can't think of a better reason to allow a large fallen Basswood tree to remain on the forest floor than that eventually a Ruffed Grouse may use it during his spring courtship ritual.

No, I am not part-owner and custodian of a "tidy" woods! Many of the branches and limbs, as well as most of the large trees, remain where they fall.

A thrilling occurrence, especially for people experiencing it the first time, is to unexpectedly flush a Ruffed Grouse when you least expect it while hiking in the woods. In reality it is they that surprise us with their deliberately-made, loud, explosive take-off. Surely this is their means of throwing natural enemies off guard for that split second it takes them to safely get away from potential danger.   So "instantly" does the bird take exit that you get little more than a glimpse of the boisterous flier.

For a long time I thought that the far-reaching drumming of a cock Ruffed Grouse would easily be heard by the "flying tiger of the night," the Great-horned Owl, who, in turn, would make a quick meal of the bird. I finally learned that the pitch of the grouse's "drum roll" is too low to be heard by the big owl. In fact a study of the stomach contents of 4,800 Great-horned Owls revealed grouse remains in less than one half of one per-cent of them.

Several years ago we were treated day after day during the grouses' spring courtship to quite a few drumming performances. Much to our joy the male chose as his drumming site an old pile of rotting logs within clear view from where we sat indoors at our kitchen table, about 150 feet away.

Once the bird became somewhat conditioned to our activities outdoors I decided to make a tape recording of one of his "concerts." Even though my field recorder is of good quality it nevertheless was incapable of picking up the low-pitched muffled "thunder" of the performer. Each booming sound was heard on my recorder's playback as a loud TICK, and nothing more.

The sound is actually produced by the sudden concussion of air filling the partial vacuum produced by the bird's extremely powerful forward, upward and finally inward wing strokes, followed by an instant reversal of the motion. Imagine the dull popping sound of an electric light bulb being dropped and broken. This is referred to as an implosion rather than an explosion and is similar, on a much smaller scale, to the marvelous sound produced by a drumming grouse.

Occasionally on our hikes into the woods we discover quite a sizable mound of grouse droppings in an opening where a lot of wild strawberries grow. Each dropping is rather cylindrical in shape, about a quarter inch in diameter and three-fourths inch long. They are composed of tiny bits of fibrous plant material. A typical mound consists of at least 20 or more droppings and most likely occurred where that grouse had spent one night under that past winter's snow.

I awoke at around 4 a.m. this morning and, as I lay awake enjoying the pre-dawn stillness, suddenly I could hear the drumming of our resident Ruffed Grouse. My estimate was that it drummed about once every minute over a period of at least 20 minutes. What interested me was that only a very small amount of skylight was visible at that early hour, although this master of percussion is known to drum to the peak of perfection throughout moonlit nights.

Given a good diversity of habitat including mature and semi-mature woods, along with middle to early successional woods having plenty of aspens and scattered with unforested openings, the Ruffed Grouse will maintain sufficient numbers to survive from year to year. Generations of people to come will thrill to this star performer whose drum rolls echo with superiority and defiance through the damp air of early spring mornings.

April Warm-Up

Two Tundra Swans rested March 26 on a sedge-meadow pond a few miles south of our place while around 20 pair of giant Canada Geese loafed on the long grassy slope nearby. A short while earlier I saw my first Pied-billed Grebe of the year on Little Lake in Sturgeon Bay.

No game bird in our state has such different "personalities" as does the Ruffed Grouse. On the one hand they can be extremely shy, flying away in an explosive roar at one's approach, while on the other hand one of these handsome creatures will virtually allow you to touch it.

The swans had their heads tucked within the feathers on their backs so I had to wait until they put their heads up before I could accurately identify them. Some Mute Swans have been in the county during the winter so, conceivably, these large white birds could have been either Mutes or Tundras.

In looking over my spring field notes and journal entries of past years it soon becomes apparent that new bird arrivals dominate the pages during most of April. As much as we patiently wait for these birds, it would be wonderful if one could have as many wildflower notes as those describing the birds.

Our huge bouquet of Balsam Poplar twigs sports shiny, light green leaves that perfume much of the house with a delicate but heady fragrance. Last Sunday, March 25, Charlotte and I needed a long hike and collected a few Leatherwood twigs on the way home. Today, Tuesday, the small yellow blossoms are already about a third out of their dark brown, fuzzy bud scales. With a little sunshine and warmth they virtually explode into flower. How I wish this handsome little native shrub, *Dirca palustris,* was more common.

The honor for the first flowering native plant in this region depends on where our hikes have taken us. If the spring has been early, sunny and warm we invariably find the first blossoming Hepaticas before the last day of March on well protected south-facing banks in our woods. The elevation at our place is around 740 feet above sea level. This puts us at approximately 160 feet above Lake Michigan, roughly four and three-fourths miles away. What a great difference this distance, and especially elevation above the cold penetrating dampness of the big lake, makes in a blossoming calendar for this region.

Should our hike take us into the low-lying Northern White Cedar swamps within sight of Lake Michigan we can in most years expect to find the first flowering plants there by around the end of the first week of April. You guessed it — the Skunk Cabbage! An early spring such as this year may bring these fascinating wildflowers into bloom a bit sooner.

Several days of sunshine are usually enough to bring the Canada Buffaloberry shrubs into flower by April tenth or even earlier in some years. Apparently these native plants do especially well when growing in a thin layer of soil over our Dolostone bedrock, more commonly referred to as Limestone by most people. One has to look closely at these unusually small one-quarter-inch flowers to realize that they actually are flowers and not the newly emerging leaves. A hand lens brings out their intricate beauty.

It's usually during the first week of April, with the maple-sap buckets still collecting "sweet water," that the first butterflies of the season appear. Any one of four can lead off the butterfly season: the Painted Lady, the Comma (one of the anglewings), Mourning Cloak or the Milbert's Tortoise-shell.

Perhaps the unusually early sighting this year, March 25, of a Turkey Vulture in southern Door County will bring about earlier-than-usual appearances of other creatures. In most years the Horned Larks are already nesting during the first week of April and Yellow-rumped Warblers can be expected no later than April 8. Fox Sparrows, the earliest of the sparrow migrants, should be here by that date too. They are transients in that they will remain for only a short time before continuing northward to their nesting grounds. My phenological records indicate that these brightly-colored sparrows seem to follow the melting snow northward. When the snow is gone, so are the Fox Sparrows.

Naturally the American Robins are the first of the thrushes to return to this region. Not only is the Hermit Thrush the earliest spring arrival of the remaining thrushes to this area, it is nearly always the last to leave in the fall. It is not uncommon to see the first Hermits of the season hunting for insects on the woodland floor before the last of the snow has melted. A good field mark to watch for is its habit of cocking its tail upward and then slowly letting it down.

The earliest spring wildflowers of April, including the Skunk Cabbage, Hepatica, Canada Buffaloberry and Leatherwood, all produce blossoms before their leaves emerge and unfurl. Another native plant that is well up by mid-April and has leaves nearly 6 to 8 inches long by April

17 is the Wild Leek. What a lovely rich green carpet they lay down in the woods long before their blossoms of mid-summer appear, the exact opposite of many other wildflowers.

By April 26 some Giant Trilliums will already be in bud and the first ones often are in flower by as early as April 28. By that time Dutchman's Breeches and a few Bellworts will also be flowering while some of the Bloodroots and Hepaticas will have already completed their blossoming. However, these are only teasers, the "April Warm-up." The really huge extravaganza of spring wildflowers will not occur until mid-May. Remember, it's always wise to warm up before a big workout!

Any wildflower that is capable of melting a tunnel through the snow in order to reach sunlight and to blossom, sometimes before the end of March, deserves our attention and admiration. Such a plant is the Skunk Cabbage. Fortunately these wildflowers of Northern White Cedar swamps and other wet woods reach their peak of unusual beauty well before the first swarms of mosquitoes come to life.

May

White Star Of The Woods

Today is that a-MAY-zing day in May when it would nearly take the combined strength of a team of draft horses to pull me away from our woods. I look outdoors this second at the smallest of the two platform bird feeders on our front lawn and see three male birds feasting there quite peaceably together, a Baltimore Oriole, Rose-breasted Grosbeak and Scarlet Tanager. Below on the ground are two male Indigo Buntings! Surrounding them in all directions are thousands of Giant-flowered Trilliums, Trout Lilies, Violets, Bellworts, Jack-in-the-pulpits and other spring wildflowers. Now do you see why it would take a team of horses to get me away from here?

An inch and a half of rain came down last night, and this morning a brisk wind whistles through the leafless woods. This will undoubtedly strip quite a few Bloodroots of their brilliant but fragile petals. I am reminded of a phrase from Robert Burns' poem, *Tam O'Shanter*, written in 1793. "But pleasures are like poppies spread, You seize the flow'r, its bloom is shed." Yes, Bloodroots are in the poppy family.

During the past few colder-than-usual weeks the emerging upright bloodroot flowers were tightly wrapped in their beautiful, strongly-veined, gray-green leaves acting for all the world like warm overcoats for warding off the cold weather. In fact it is common for the large foliage of these "white stars" of the woodland to remain unopened until after the petals have fallen.

Their upright streamlined seedpods will eventually contain round chestnut-brown seeds. A fascinating feature of these Bloodroot seeds, as well as other wildflower seeds, is the drapery of white tissue on a part of their outer surface when they fall to the ground. This material, called elaiosome (e-LIE-o-soam), contains among other substances certain vital lipids which the lowly ants that gather them cannot synthesize from other foods available to them in the wild.

Lipids, in general, combined with proteins and carbohydrates, constitute the principal structural components of living cells. The seeds are gathered by the ants and carried into their underground nests where the elaiosome is removed from the seeds, chewed into pieces and fed to the ant larvae. Call it baby food if you wish!

Now comes the unsuspected miracle. The seeds, having been cleaned of the elaisome, are hauled by the ants to the colony's dump heap, most likely located on top of the underground chamber, or buried nearby on the forest floor along with the corpses from the colony. Studies have proven that the ant-distributed seeds grow much better than those dropped naturally from the bursting seed pods onto the ground below. In fact in some cases it was only the seeds buried by the ants that germinated and eventually produced flowers.

Upon analyzing the so-called "compost heaps" of the ants it was found that they contained a wonderful balance of nitrogen, phosphorus and potassium, precisely the elements found in commercially produced fertilizers used on vegetable and flower gardens and on farmers' crops.

Those seeds collected and eaten by White-footed Mice, for example, are "goners" and are naturally destroyed. If it weren't for the often-despised ants we wouldn't have nearly the exquisite, flamboyant carpet of wildflowers enjoyed each spring by so many people. Now there! Doesn't this make you "antsy" for your first picnic in the woods?

Back to the Bloodroot which the Ojibwe people of this region called "meskwa dji bikuk" (red root) and of which they used the root to cure, among other ailments, sore throats. The orange-red

Large-flowered Trilliums, like many other wild plants and animals, can vary considerably in size. The palm of my hand is three and one-half inches wide and will help you to visualize how unusually large this specimen was. This large form of a trillium continues to be of bigger-than-normal size every year.

juice was squeezed out of the root onto a lump of maple sugar, then retained in the mouth until the sugar had melted away. Bear in mind that the thin, reddish, latex-like sap in the rhizome contains several alkaloids which may be quite poisonous, depending upon how much is used.

 The juice was also used to paint the face for the medicine lodge ceremony, or when on the warpath. This reminds me of a group of my junior high students who nearly went on the "war path" one time. I had taken them into the spring woods to learn about the ephemeral wildflowers, those that come and go quickly. Actually we had a great deal of fun, an activity those strongly peer-oriented youngsters related to extremely well.

First I would locate a large patch of several dozen Bloodroots then dig down to secure a two or three-inch root. Slicing through the root with a sharp jackknife caused it to ooze forth with a very bloody-looking substance. Demonstrating, I carefully and artistically decorated the face of one of the "brave" students. Next I provided each of the pupils with a short section of the brilliant root and told them to "Go to it!" Within minutes they resembled a band of genuine ancient Native Americans on the war path!

Now came the shocker. I gently informed them that it would take at least a week for the dye to wear off. Had those unnaturalized warring "Native Americans" possessed hatchets I surely would have lost my scalp! What I didn't tell them was that a little soap and water would easily remove the war paint. I did find out the next morning which kids washed their faces before coming to school!

If one were to travel to some of the off-the-beaten-track places out east and question the people there about this striking white flower in their woods they would most likely call it Tetterwort, Red Puccoon, redroot, red Indian paint, corn root, termeric or sweet slumber, all tantalizing colloquialisms every bit as meaningful as our bloodroot name.

Their finger-thick, fleshy, perennial rootstalks aided by the large pancake-size leaves slowly accumulate nourishment as the flowering season progresses, continuing well into summer. Come autumn, the plant will have built up sufficient food in its root to enable the flower to emerge very early the following spring as the first hint of warmth and moisture are felt, a few weeks before the trees' canopy of leaves has formed. What dazzling jewels these white stars weave into the spring woods' tapestry!

Wildflower Parade

There is a wildflower that appears to defy cold, rainy, even snowy April days, the Hepatica. This hardy native is at its best on sunny days.

Its genus and best common name are the same, *Hepatica.* Even though *Gray's Manual of Botany* refers only to the Trailing Arbutus as Mayflower, many people in this region mean Hepaticas when they mention Mayflowers. Actually, if the month of its first heavy blooming were important in its naming, they should be called Aprilflowers.

The sequence of wildflower blossoming is bound to differ slightly from woods to woods, county to county, and will be affected by elevations of the growing site and nearness to cold "refrigerative" bodies of water.

In general, one can assume that spring advances northward about 125 miles per week. A blossoming calendar faithfully kept from year to year (phenological record) can vary considerably. Favorite spring ephemerals (short-lived to coincide with the brief spell of sun-drenched soil before tree-leaf canopy forms) include Hepatica, Bloodroot, Trout Lily, Dutchman's Breeches, Squirrel Corn, Spring Beauty, Marsh Marigold, Wood Anemone, Bellwort, Toothwort, Jack-in-the-pulpit,

Trilliums, Meadow-Rue, Canada Mayflower, various Violets, Mayapple, Bishop's Cap and Solomon's Seal.

Very likely I learned the name, Hepatica, from my Mother who knew the wildflowers well. *Gray's Manual of Botany* lists two species. *Acutiloba* (a-cue-ti-LOW-ba), having pointed leaf lobes and bracts, tends to be more western and favors dry to medium woods with limy soil. This species bears staminate flowers on one plant and pistillate on another.

The other species, *americana,* bears flowers of both sexes above the roots. They have rounded leaf lobes and bracts and are more likely to grow in acid soil. However, both do nicely on partially shaded slopes and in rocky terrain where the woods are rich in leaf-mold. In fact both species have been found existing very well in the same woods.

Another of its names, Liverleaf, is well chosen because its genus name, *Hepatica*, is related to the word liver. *Hepaticus* (Latin) pertains to liver as does the Greek name, *hepar*. Examine a leaf and you will see its liver shape.

Last year's leaves, fleshy, leathery, maroon to rusty-olive, lie matted on the forest floor as the new flowers unfold. New leaves, fuzzy and heart-shaped at the base, make their appearance as the long-lasting flowers wither.

People of many years ago religiously believed in that ancient "Doctrine of Signatures" whereby portions of plants resembling some organ of the body, for example, would prove to be beneficial in curing ailments of that organ. Naturally the leaves of Hepaticas were thought to be an antidote for liver complications – which in reality they most certainly were not.

The range of these flowers is extensive stretching from northern Florida and Alabama north to Nova Scotia and Manitoba, and west into Minnesota. They also inhabit Alaska and Europe. A different species, *H. angulosa*, having large white, blue or reddish flowers, is native to Hungary. God must have loved the Hepaticas, He made so many of them.

Like usual we enjoy our woods to the hilt every year on Mayday. A special point is made to look for Hepaticas of different colors. Based upon past experiences, and from an unusually early

A very long blooming season is enjoyed by Hepaticas, extending some springs in eastern Wisconsin from the last week of March well into the middle of May. Those growing in the deciduous woods near the shores of the colder Lake Michigan naturally are the last to bloom while some of the sunny, south-facing openings in more inland woods occasionally surprise us with these delicate pastel flowers before all the snow has melted.

blooming date of March 23 one year, they will range from nearly pure white to pastel shades of blue, purple and pink. The deep blues capture our fancy while the rich pinks are undoubtedly the rarest in our woods.

It is nearly an insult to tell people that Hepaticas have no petals. Rather they sport showy sepals that are petal-like. Some botanists refer to them as tepals. Examining a flowering plant in more detail, you will discover three tiny unlobed leaves, often mistaken for sepals, immediately below the "technically real" colorful sepals. You will also find that a short flower stalk, or peduncle, separates these leaves from the flower.

The blossoms of these vernal favorites close at night, then open again the next sunny or bright day. Densely overcast days will find them tightly shut and unavailable. Study several clumps of them daily and try to determine for how many days one flower remains open.

Their odor is faint but sweet, and some tend to lack fragrance entirely. There are those wildflower devotees who claim that the sweetest-scented Hepatica clusters this year will be just as sweet next year.

Hepaticas are worthy of more praise and study. In fact its entire family, the Crowfoot family (alluding to the leaf shape), is one of unusual beauty and includes over 30 species of Buttercups, Meadow-Rue, Anemone, Clematis (pronounced CLEM-a-tis), Delphinium, Marsh Marigold, Columbine and Baneberry.

For those of you who have a woodlot and many Hepaticas, I'd like to suggest a way of beating spring to the punch next year. Come late September, dig a few Hepatica plants you have marked, put them in large clay pots, cover with leaf mulch, place in your coldframe and leave them there through the first half of winter. Bring them indoors any time after mid-winter where they will bloom quickly in a sunny window offering you a sneak preview of spring. Naturally those plants, following blossoming, can be replanted in your woods once the soil thaws.

I would be the happiest person alive if all elementary and secondary curricula, public and private as well, would make it mandatory for every student during every year of their schooling to learn something about plants, wildflowers, vegetables and flowers, the soil and the wonderful art of growing, caring for and enjoying the flowering world.

Even though its music is soft and delicate, the message of this wildflower parade comes through loudly and clearly. The tiny size of these spring ephemerals marches in step with towering enjoyment for those who wish to find it. Once found, never let it go. Do everything in your power to preserve forever this wild garden of unmatched beauty.

Master Carpenter

There occasionally comes a very pleasant surprise while leisurely enjoying the May woods filled with wildflowers. Suddenly you discover a large halo of fresh wood chips encircling the base of a huge American Beech tree and you immediately know who has, within the past several weeks, excavated a new nesting cavity somewhere "up there," a Pileated Woodpecker.

Nest construction of these crow-size woodpeckers sometimes begins well before all the snow has melted. It's also the season to hear the start of the male's "advertising campaign." His deep resonant drumming will carry for a half-mile or more on a still day and his loud, harsh "cuk cuk cuk cuk cuk" notes will ring with authority through the woods.

What a perfect genus name the Pileated has, *Dryocopus* (dry-OCK-o-pus)—taken from the Greek meaning "tree cleaver." Its species name is *pileatus* (pie-leh-AY-tus) based upon the Latin word "pileum" (PIE-le-um) meaning cap. We prefer to pronounce the bird's name, "PIE-le-ay-ted" whereby others call it "PIL-le-ay-ted." Both are accepted. I also enjoy one of the bird's nicknames, "Good God Woodpecker," given to this awesome creature by mountain people of the East.

The nesthole, dug mostly by the female, may take upwards of 30 days to complete. Examine the inside of one and you will agree that it is quite a work of art, not rough and slivery as one might expect but rather smooth to the touch.

Don't confuse a feeding excavation with a nesthole entrance. I've seen trees where a Pileated Woodpecker, in its quest for carpenter ants or larvae of wood-boring beetles, such as Horntails, made holes that were six inches wide, at least that deep and as much as three feet long. The nest entrance is usually rectangular in shape and approximately 3 ☐ inches by 4 inches in size. The inside cavity will average about 19 inches deep.

It is thought that the vibrations of the insects within what appears to be a perfectly sound tree, or possibly the strong odor of formic acid given off by the carpenter ants, serve as targets at which "Piley" aims his attack. The barbed tongue tip, coated with a sticky substance, is thought to be highly alkaline, perfect for neutralizing the strong formic acid of the ants.

Many observations have confirmed the fact that older, unused Pileated nesting and roosting cavities are later taken over and used as nestholes by Wood Ducks, Common Goldeneye Ducks, Common Flickers, Screech Owls and Great Crested Flycatchers as well as Flying Squirrels. Now you can realize the great importance of the Pileated's "house-building" for other wildlife.

Its short strong legs, curved, needle-sharp claws, thick shock-absorbing skull, and very stiff tail feathers, used as a prop against a tree, all serve this wily bird well.

With a fairly close look it's easy to distinguish the male from the female. The "mustache" patch extending from the base of the bill backward is all black on the female. The male's mustache patch contains some red feathers. Also the entire crest of the male is red whereas only the back half of the female's is red.

One of my most interesting observations of a Pileated Woodpecker took place at Toft Point several years ago. I could hear a woodpecker working ahead of me as I quietly hiked toward the

This Pileated Wood-pecker and Black-capped Chickadee appeared to be quite comfortable feasting on the beef suet within inches of one another, true "partners in nature." The slow lumbering flight of this largest of Wisconsin woodpeckers makes it a fairly easy target for its natural predators including the Northern Goshawk and Cooper's Hawk. Unquestionably the shyness and extreme wariness of this crow-sized woodpecker can be attributed to its vulnerability.

buildings. Finally I spied "Piley" working near the base of a large Arborvitae tree. Apparently the meal was too good to abandon just because I had arrived on the scene, so I was lucky to be able to watch him for two or three minutes from within forty feet.

Now came the surprise. The woodpecker became impatient with my presence and flew into the nearby woods. Within seconds a couple of Black-capped Chickadees, a Red-breasted Nuthatch and a Downy Woodpecker, the "clean-up crew," took over where "Piley" had left off. What a thorough going-over the dinner table received. Not a single crumb would be wasted as these efficient gleaners went about their work.

Here's to the master carpenter of all US birds, the gold medal winner, the Pileated Woodpecker!

Red-Eyed Minstrels

For quite a few years it was thought that the American Redstart, Ovenbird and Red-eyed Vireo were the three most abundant bird species in the deciduous forests of eastern North America, totaling in the millions of individual birds. By 1965 the population of the Red-eyed Vireo was already beginning to "crash," and since then their population has been steadily decreasing.

It is always a thrill to hear our first Red-eyed Vireo each May on our property, and it is likely that the male will saturate the woods with his day-long singing for the rest of the summer. This five-inch-long bird makes up for its easy-to-hear, never-ending vocalizations by being downright maddening to locate in the tree tops by birdwatchers.

Wilson Flagg, student of birds some years ago nicknamed it the "preacher bird," and rightly so. A Canadian ornithologist, L. de Kirline, studied one Red-eyed Vireo for an entire day and learned that it sang 22,197 songs during that time! What an endless sermon! Assuming that southern Canada might have 20 hours of daylight in June, that would amount to about 16 or 17 songs per minute. What vocal power!

Were it not for this bird's continuous singing it would go quite unnoticed, for its colors blend perfectly with the forest canopy – olives, grays, whites and yellows. The rich rusty-red iris of this handsome bird can be detected only from fairly close range and under good light conditions.

Its dark grayish crown is set off by a black marginal line and a white line over the eye. There are no wing bars and the bird's underparts are whitish. A close look will reveal a rather heavy bill very slightly hooked at the tip. In fact the bird is considered to be a relative to the larger Logger-head Shrike that has a distinctly hooked beak.

One would think that the name, *Vireo*, is related to its song whereas in reality its Latin derivation means "to be green." The common names of very few birds are the same as their scientific names such as the vireo.

The vireo's song would be a perfect example of an allegro movement in a symphony – brisk. It is a choppy, high-pitched, rapid roundelay sung in clear tones. Exactly what this incessant musician is trying to say is hard to understand. Perhaps it is constantly broadcasting its territorial claims, strengthening a pair-bond, releasing nervous energy, or just plain practicing. Maybe the best guess is simply that vireos love to sing!

One of the finest descriptions of the Red-eyed Vireo's monotonous song was set to the English language also by Wilson Flagg. He could hear one repeating over and over, "You see it...you know it…do you hear me?…do you believe it?"

The Red-eyed Vireo surely must be ranked among those birds that are persistent singers, easy-to-hear, but unusually difficult to locate. It is often in the uppermost leafy crowns of decidu-ous trees that these birds hunt for insects, further causing them to be well hidden from view of most birdwatchers.

Several years ago some friends shared with Charlotte and me a very precious discovery. Chuck had been pruning small limbs mostly from American Beech trees growing along their narrow driveway through the woods. He was just about to lop off a small branch at eye level when he fortunately noticed a delicate basket-like nest suspended from a forked twig and occupied by a little beady-eyed bird.

Three white eggs with a small amount of dark brownish speckles were in the well-made nest. The amazing tameness of the adult bird was quite unbelievable. Literature indicates that nesting vireos have been gently lifted off the nest and set back into place without fleeing in fright.

The bird, either male or female because both are known to incubate, and both are identical in color, lived up to our friends' descriptions of trust and patience. With the side door of Chuck's van opened wide I kneeled down, steadied my camera against the door frame within five feet of the nest, and took several pictures of the precious little bird. Not once did it flinch or show fright.

Its pendulous nest is skillfully constructed from dried grass, fibers from vines and other plants, bits of paper, thin strips of Paper Birch bark, mosses, lichens, leaves and even bits of paper from wasps nests. Fine plant materials, white pine needles, or even hair, line this exquisite masterpiece.

The nests of few species of birds on the entire continent are parasitized as much by the Brown-headed Cowbirds as those of the Red-eyed Vireos. It is a fairly common sight to see the diminutive vireo adults feeding one or more young cowbirds that are about twice the size of the parents. One study of 114 vireo nests revealed that 87 had been parasitized by cowbirds, about 75%.

These indefatigable singers also spend many hours devouring great quantities of injurious insects, especially span worms and leaf rollers. Several types of fruits, such as dogwood and Virginia Creeper, are included along with scores of caterpillars, moths, flies, beetles and spiders.

Our lives have been made richer by our eye-to-eye visits with the trustful Red-eyed Vireos. These little minstrels of the treetops, the birds that outlast nearly all other birds in the singing department, have stressed once more how valuable birds are to nature – as well as to people!

Fearless Plover

A few years ago a bird weighing about 3 1/2 ounces fearlessly protected its eggs from the unsuspecting feet of 21 adults totaling at least 3500 pounds.

I was in the lead car of a caravan of five that drove onto a Dolostone flat of "glacial pavement" to begin our outdoor class of geology and fossils. Even before I had turned off the engine the Killdeer was up and running.

The first thing that entered my mind was to rush outside and warn the others to watch where every foot went down – so that they wouldn't accidentally step on the eggs. By now the adult bird had "broken" its wings and was helplessly and painfully floundering on the bedrock within 50 feet of where we stood, trying its best to distract us from the only things it owned in the entire world, its eggs.

Unknowingly the people had excitedly left their cars to begin looking at the glacial scratches and abundant fossils. Fortunately one of the people in my car had quickly discovered the well-camouflaged eggs, and I alerted everyone in the group.

Now began one of the most courageous demonstrations I have ever seen in the animal world. With all 21 people lined up for a better view of the nest, that fearless bird raced toward us and

A close look at a Killdeer, its wing feathers and tail stiffly spread in protection of the bird's clutch of eggs, reveals some fascinating feather shapes. This Killdeer refused to budge as it courageously guarded its eggs on the 23rd day of incubation. The photograph was taken, using a 500-mm telephoto lens, from a distance of approximately 14 feet.

defiantly stood next to its nest, screaming to the top of its lungs, daring us to take one more step toward its priceless possession, its four eggs. The line of people was within five feet of the bird.

A few people with cameras approached the courageous Killdeer to within three feet for pictures. Undaunted, the lion-hearted bird stood its ground, protecting the fragile eggs from the big people's feet.

Not having had a camera that day for close-ups, I returned the following day to record on film the fearless little creature. Now neither bird so much as uttered their piercing alarm calls. They were nearby but obviously didn't sense the great danger presented by the larger group of people the day before.

I have a hunch that the Killdeer, seeing 21 huge humans lined up and walking toward its nest, sensed that the only act that would save the eggs from destruction would be to fly directly to the nest and let the people actually see where the eggs were.

Assume that the average person in this group weighed approximately 700 times more than the Killdeer. Now put this incident into an entirely different and somewhat farfetched perspective. Imagine a tiny, helpless, 18-pound human infant lying on the ground while a herd of 21 colossal bull Elephants, each weighing 13,000 pounds, moved slowly toward the child.

The adult is 700 times the size of the Killdeer while one Elephant is roughly that many times heavier than an infant child. I find it hard to imagine a parent of that child brave enough to protectively stand guard, to ward off 21 Elephants.

Indeed, that tiny Killdeer had "what it takes!" Perhaps if all our worldly possessions were whittled down to one thing, like the Killdeers eggs, we too would risk death in protecting that valuable asset.

The relatively large size of the Killdeer eggs and the fact that they require about 25 days of incubation before hatching is related to the large size of the hatched birds. Like baby chickens and Ruffed Grouse, they are precotial (pre-COE-shul) and can within minutes after hatching be running with mama and papa.

Both adults take turns incubating the large, rather pointed, dull, protectively-colored eggs. Nature provided the Killdeer with pointed eggs so that they roll in a very small arc, easily staying together in this very open nest upon the ground.

The youngest baby Killdeers I've ever seen reminded me of marshmallows stuck onto toothpicks. But could they ever scoot in search of insects.

I shall always remember an experience of watching a family of four very tiny baby Killdeers searching for insects in the wet grass on a cold July morning. The frigid air was more than they could stand for very long, and about every minute they'd scurry back to mama and duck beneath her feathers for warmth, then back out for more insect catching.

What continues to greatly impress me are the Killdeers' (and other birds') absolute simple requirements for living. A hot arid dolostone flat for their nest and scores of insects to eat including beetles, grasshoppers, ants and flies fulfill their basic needs. Apparently these birds obtain sufficient moisture from the insects they eat, judging by the birds' considerable distance from water.

What wonderful enjoyment and lessons for our own lives come from the Killdeer, a bird that does nothing whatever to damage the environment. What fine examples they offer for us to follow!

June

Slow But Snappy

Those leisurely four-legged reptiles with the toothless smiles are on the loose, the turtles. June would not be normal if a group of us hikers wouldn't surprise at least a half dozen females seriously preoccupied with their all-important egg-laying.

Several people and I were thoroughly startled a few days ago. We had just finished looking at an unusual plant within sight of a swampy wetland, turned away to continue our walk and suddenly found ourselves momentarily startled, caught off guard, staring face to face with a monstrous turtle.

I'm sure this huge weather-beaten grandmother (many times over!) of a Snapping Turtle with green algae growing on her back would have been too large to fit in the bottom of a bushel basket. No one in the group including myself was about to pick up the ponderous creature to estimate its weight. My guess is that it would have tipped the scales at about 30 pounds or more. Fifteen is said to be average but records of over 50 pounds are known.

A Box Turtle, living in the wild, was proven to be 138 years old. Do you suppose that this gigantic snapper, queen of the swamps, was already here before the first white settlers of the 1850's? It would be interesting to know how many times she has laid eggs.

This female Painted Turtle, head and legs firmly tucked beneath her carapace, had just finished laying her clutch of eggs in early June. Now she would have a journey of at least 300 yards to the nearest body of water. Weighting down a chicken-wire cage over the nesting site will protect the eggs from being eaten by typical predators such as a skunk or raccoon. Depending on weather conditions and other variable factors, the young may not leave their buried nest site until the following May or June.

One of the people in our group said, "How in the world can such a slow-moving female ever attract a male?" Nature has taken this into account by enabling females of many turtle species to lay fertile eggs for several consecutive years after a single mating.

Naturally I had no camera when we happened onto the unhurried giant. The only evidence I could find of her whereabouts the next day was three shallow pits on the nearby sandy rise where she had attempted to lay her eggs. All one could hope for is that predators, such as raccoons, foxes or skunks, would not dig up and eat the eggs. They are white, quite spherical and about one inch in diameter.

Unfortunately many humans have come to the conclusion that Snapping Turtles are of little economic importance other than supplying the basic ingredient for turtle soup. I would strongly disagree with this attitude. In the first place we do not know nearly enough about these animals to reach a final resolution. It is a well-known fact that they eat some ducklings and game fish, but who is to say that ducks and fish are more important in the natural environment than turtles?

It is a proven fact that most turtles consume scores of injurious slugs, snails, insects, and far more aquatic plants than has previously been suspected. Hopefully there will always be sluggish waters with mucky bottoms, areas unfit for human habitation (at least as long as those areas are not drained or filled in) where the prudent snappers can safely survive.

I enjoyed a "stare down" with a Midland Painted Turtle one time. The sky was clear and sunny and I was walking on a narrow footbridge across a shallow pond. Suddenly I saw the olive-black turtle slip off the half-submerged log and into the water-lily pond.

I hurried to the rim of the pond, sat on the edge of the wooden footbridge, and watched for the faintest movement of aquatic plants. Nearly a minute had elapsed before I caught sight of the cautious turtle submerged beneath a leaf. Fortunately I had my watch along and could time the entire episode. It was 10 minutes before the shy six-inch-long animal barely broke the surface of the water with its two tiny nostrils and took a breath. Four minutes later it crawled onto the log to resume its sunbath. Being cold-blooded creatures, Painted Turtles spend much time basking.

Even though I tried to be motionless, it was either the sight or odor of me, or perhaps both, that did not appeal to the turtle. Into the shallow pond it dove and swam surprisingly quickly to the far end.

Surely one of the most amazing features of a turtle is its shell. It has been said that if a person were proportionately as strong as the shell of a Box Turtle they could support two large African Elephants. Little wonder that these amazing reptiles, who carry their "houses" on their backs, have been so successful in surviving through the years and can live to such an old age.

Our Summer Squirrel

One of these days I'm going to recreate a little refuge along the edge of our front yard, in view from our dining room window, similar to the one that provided us with so much animal entertainment in our former home. The refuge I speak of is nothing more than a woodpile.

The one that previously had become such an important part of our lives was stacked against the east side of the woodshed and was about four feet high and eight feet long. Fifteen-inch-long chunks of White Spruce were piled in such a way that many of the spaces between the pieces of wood were large enough for the small animals to crawl into.

Seven species of rodents, one carnivore and one insectivore, most likely among others, used the woodpile for various reasons according to our observations. The rodents included the Red Squirrel, Flying Squirrel, Gray Squirrel, Eastern Chipmunk, 13-lined Spermophile, Meadow Vole

Much like the "big" fish that got away, many people would tend to exaggerate the true length of a 13-Lined Spermophile. Standing upright on their short hind legs and stretching their "stripes" as long as possible, their total length is no more than 11 inches from the tip of their nose to the end of their four and one-half-inch-long tail.

and White-footed Mouse. The carnivore was the Short-tailed Weasel while the insectivore was the Short-tailed Shrew.

The 13-lined Spermophile, also referred to as the Gopher or Ground Squirrel (one of several species in the US), used the woodpile mainly as a temporary retreat. There is where it frequently hid when suddenly scared from its sunflower feasting place beneath the nearby bird feeders.

People often confuse the Gopher with the Chipmunk. They are quite similar in size but vary considerably in body shape, color pattern and mannerisms. If the animal scampers away from you with its tail parallel to the ground it is most likely a Gopher. Chipmunks invariably carry theirs vertically during their speedy get-away. Gophers have no stripes on their cheeks as do Chipmunks.

A Gopher does have 13 pale buff stripes and 12 dark stripes adorning its back. Five of the lighter stripes are a series of buffy dots. This striking pattern of light and dark stripes and spots provides this vulnerable mammal with camouflage against its many natural enemies including the Red-tailed Hawk, Gray and the Red Foxes, Badger, Weasel, house cat, Northern Harrier and snake. Harriers with their superb sight and Badgers with their extraordinary digging powers prey upon them quite heavily.

Gophers can easily trick you into thinking their bodies are more than six to seven inches long. Standing upright on their short hind legs and stretching their "stripes" as long as possible they lead one to exaggerate in describing their total length. Actually it is no more than 11 inches from the tip of its nose to the end of its four and a half-inch long tail.

Its narrow conical-shaped head is somewhat smaller than a Chipmunk's and it has less storage space in its cheek pouches. It has very small ears and conspicuous light eye rings. The claws on the four toes of its forefeet are quite long while those on its hind toes are short and strong.

Every state in its large range surely has a dozen or more colloquial names for this common rodent including striper, grass chippie, leopard ground squirrel, striped gopher and whistle sneak.

One of its most interesting names is the federation squirrel in allusion to its 13 stripes and several stars.

Their food consists mostly of animal matter supplemented with seeds, grain, berries and nuts. Grasshoppers, June Beetles, cutworms and crickets are among their favorite foods. Because of their long hibernation they generally do not harm stored crops. However, they are known to do some damage to certain grains such as very young corn as well as garden vegetables including beets, peas, beans and melons.

Our best guess is that Gophers inhabiting this cold lakeshore region near the 45th parallel spend about five months above the ground and seven months below the ground in hibernation. My first sighting of one this year was on April 26. The end of September into the middle of October is about as late as we have observed them here. This comes out to around five and a half months.

Their body temperature in summer reaches around 105 degrees F. while their heartbeat can go up to as many as 400 per minute. Come winter their body temperature drops to a few degrees above freezing and their heartbeat drops to as low as five or fewer per minute. Fat accumulated during the summer months, when their weight doubles from May to September, is slowly burned, thereby supplying them with the very small amount of energy they need to remain alive.

These rather unsociable 13-lined Spermophiles have one annual litter of around nine young. The adult female has 10 mammae. Babies grow rapidly and are full-grown by three months, living to as much as five years. Were it not that they are so heavily preyed upon, the Great Plains and the Midwest would have Ground Squirrels coming out of their ears!

We look at them as belonging to that great kingdom of wild animals existing together in a complicated but wonderful system of checks and balances. These sprightly spermophiles will always be accepted in our yard as long as they don't "gopher" the baby beets in the garden!

Winged Jewels

It's been a fascinating spring thus far, especially observing the emergence of wildflowers and the arrival of migratory birds. Yes, farmers, orchardists and gardeners desperately need rain and so do the native herbaceous and woody plants. The American Robins on our property, in need of nest-building materials, have learned that there is always plenty of mud and mossy plants to be had around the bird baths that we have set upon the ground, the birds' favorites.

Several of the first arriving birds this spring, such as Red-winged Blackbirds and Common Grackles, were already in the region a week or two earlier than usual. Woodland wildflowers came into bloom two full weeks earlier than in most years, but strangely the northward migrations of many songbirds were not affected by El Niño as were the wildflowers and the leafing out of trees.

In fact birdwatchers from throughout the state wondered what happened to the warblers earlier this month. Very few were seen. The general thought is that most of the warblers, thrushes, and also White-throated and White-crowned Sparrows either made very brief stops in the region or went straight on through to their northern nesting grounds without lingering here as they usually do.

The arrival date of the Ruby-throated Hummingbirds at our place this year, May 16, was only two days earlier than last year. All 72 counties in Wisconsin lay claim to nesting rubythroats, one of the most well loved and frequently observed songbirds in the state. Surely the flowers that are used in landscaping around homes, and also the common practice of supplying these tiny "winged jewels" with sugar-water feeders have contributed to attracting so many of these birds to the yards of people's homes.

We noticed only one male rubythroat at our feeders on Saturday, May 16. By the next day another male had joined the scene, and now the aerial "battle" began. Occasionally the two birds would momentarily rest, perhaps catching their breaths, on the two thin perches I fastened to the porch railing-supports, one on each side of the upper level feeder.

Later on Sunday, the 17th, a female hummer arrived on the scene, and now the two little male "spitfires" really stepped up their attacks on one another. They were so totally concentrated on one another's position that I was able to crank open the east kitchen window, set up my tripod and camera inside the kitchen within eight feet from where they perched near the feeder, and snap one picture after another. They couldn't have cared less!

By Monday the 18th only one male, the victor, remained at the feeders. The other had left for more peaceful surroundings. Unfortunately we haven't seen the female either, but that doesn't surprise us in the slightest. In past years the male did everything in his power to "hog" the feeders and would continually drive the female away from them. In this case a person should place hummingbirds feeders on opposite sides of the house, thereby making it impossible for the male hummer to see more than one feeder at a time.

 Surprisingly hummingbirds comprise one of the largest of all bird families, around 320+ species, all of which are confined to the New World. Twelve species breed in the continental US while the great majority are to be found in South America. Even though a few stragglers, such as Anna's Hummingbird, occasionally nest east of the Mississippi River, it is usually assumed that only the Ruby-throated nests in this large region.

This incredible little bird's dazzling iridescent colors, as seen in the sunlight, range from ruby-red to violet, green, blue, bronze, gold and yellow. Added to its awesome appearance are its fascinating behavior as well as several benefits to people such as pollinating flowers and eating countless tiny insects. Little wonder they are so popular with humans. By the way, the male's so-called gorget (colorful throat patch) contains no red pigment but rather refracts, then reflects its ruby-red to our eyes via the sunlight. In the shade the throat patch is black.

Several hummingbird feeders, strategically placed near windows for good viewing, invariably lead the daily watchers into admitting that no other species of bird brings them as much day-to-day, summer enjoyment and satisfaction. It is usually during late July and into August that sightings of one of the Clear-wing Moths, hovering and drinking nectar at their petunias and other flowers, leads people to believe they are seeing a different species of hummingbird.

I've read in several reference books of various ways to prepare the sugar solution to be fed to the hummers. In the first place, never use honey, only the typical white cane sugar. The recommended ratio is one part sugar to four parts water. A serious mistake can be made by allowing the sugar and water to boil too long, thereby providing the hummingbirds with a sugar-water solution that is too sweet. The thought is that this can lead to damaged livers in the birds.

The method I prefer is to mix one part sugar to one part water, then bring that to a boil. By boiling it you completely dissolve the sugar and you also reduce the chances of fungus building up in the feeders that, in turn, can be harmful to the birds. Now you mix one part of this mixture with four parts water. Store that which you don't use immediately in the refrigerator. It is further recommended that, once the hummers become conditioned to using the feeders, you reduce the mixture to one part sugar (the one-to-one blend) to six parts water. This will insure little chance of liver damage for the birds and also force them into eating more natural foods.

Planting bright-colored tubular flowers, especially orange and yellow, along with Columbine, Bee Balm, Butterfly Milkweed, Trumpet Vine, Coralbells, Hollyhocks, Nasturtiums, Petunias, Phlox and Zinnias will both attract the hummers and also provide them with food. Bear in mind that nectar from the flowers or your sugar-water feeders provides these birds with around one-fourth of their food. The remaining three-fourths comes from the insects that they find especially in the tubular flowers.

Are you convinced as we are that the petite one-tenth of one ounce Ruby-throated Hummingbird is the most precious, fascinating bird in all of eastern United States?

Fabulous Ferns

What a delightful 33 and a half-minute walk I had early this morning along the off-the-beaten-track gravel road near our home. I'm trying to work off some of my "gluteus flabulose" excess baggage by walking a two-mile course at a brisk pace while continuously swinging my arms. My pulse at the end of the outing was 120. Hopefully I will reduce time, weight and pulse before the year comes to an end.

First a pair of Sandhill Cranes bugled as they flew over the newly planted fields along the way, and then some Northern Ravens provided me with a most wonderful sunrise concert of marvelous conversational notes. Rose-breasted Grosbeaks and Baltimore Orioles seemed to be singing from all directions adding a "symphonic accompaniment" to the walk.

I couldn't help but notice some fern "fiddleheads" poking their way out of the forest floor along the route. These graceful plants, among my favorites, made their appearance on Earth during the Carboniferous Period, also referred to as the Age of Ferns, which began around 260 million years ago and lasted for about 25 million years.

Young fronds emerging from the ground appear as tightly coiled crosiers. Because they resemble violin scrolls, people for centuries have called them fiddleheads. Bear in mind that there is no such thing as a specific "fiddlehead fern." Practically all ferns begin their growth in spring rising out of the ground and appearing like fiddleheads.

Some people in this country, particularly in the northeastern states, eat the young developing fiddleheads of several species and prepare them much like asparagus. Unfortunately it was determined a few years ago that the crosiers (fiddlehead stage) of Bracken Ferns are carcinogenic. The latest word is that no fern fiddleheads are safe to eat, that consuming them can possibly lead

I shall never forget experiencing the many enormous 15 to 20-foot-wide circular patches of Maidenhair Ferns growing in the area of the sacred Native American burial grounds on Garden Island, in upper Lake Michigan about 40 miles west of the Mackinac Bridge. One after another, these gentle imposing gardens of ferns decorate this hushed primeval setting. That memorable occasion added greatly to my deep love for this elegant plant.

to cancer. As to contaminants in things people eat, it has been said that "living is hazardous to your health!"

The extremely abundant and widespread Bracken Ferns clothe the mountain slopes of Scotland as well as hundreds of miles of roadsides throughout much of Wisconsin especially where it is not too shady. Dairy cattle that are overgrazed in woodlands, where the available greens are never very abundant, will eventually be forced to turn to the large triangular three-parted fronds of these ferns. If this occurs, especially during the latter part of the growing season, overindulgence will kill the cows.

One of the best known ferns in eastern Wisconsin is the Maidenhair, distinctive, delicate and extremely beautiful. The nearly circular blade is attached to a deep purplish-brown stipe (stem of a fern). Look closely and you will see a funnel-form in the center radiating horizontally toward the perimeter, elegant and graceful.

Charlotte and I hiked into one of the hidden, unknown botanical gems of northeastern Wisconsin yesterday, a large acid bog containing, among other unusual plants, several acres of Leatherleaf, Bog Laurel, Wintergreen, Labrador Tea, Blueberry, Bog Rosemary and Wild Cranberry. Two ferns in their crosier stage immediately caught our eye, the large shrub-like Royal Fern and the Cinnamon Fern, two species that prefer to have their feet in cold, acidy, moist ground.

A feature of most ferns that I especially enjoy is the rather demanding set of growing conditions for each particular species. Three that do very well in thin layers of moss on dolostone in cool humid environments are the Maidenhair Spleenwort, Green Spleenwort and the Rock-cap or Common Polypody. All are quite fragile and should be looked at and enjoyed—but not touched.

Quite a few of the 82 species of ferns in Wisconsin (not including 20 hybrids) have fascinating and descriptive names. The Sensitive Fern is sensitive to the first killing frost of autumn and will turn brown overnight. Individual tiny leaflets of the Christmas Fern, rare in the state but appearing in a few sites in Door County, appear like miniature Christmas stockings "hung by the fireplace."

You may have what are called Asparagus Ferns growing in your home. Like the Spanish Moss of the South, which is actually not a moss, these Asparagus "Ferns" are members of the pineapple family along with the Spanish Moss, have flowers and reproduce by seeds in spite of their looking much like lacy ferns.

Buy yourself a hand-lens and a little fern field guide, such as the pocket-sized *Fern Finder* by Anne C. and Barbara G. Hallowell (Nature Study Guild). Become familiar with such fern terms as frond, blade, stipe, rachis, pinna and pinnule. You'll be amazed at how easy it is to learn the relatively small number of fern species of your county, perhaps between 20 and 30. Door County, for example, has 28 species, not including several hybrids.

Add a new dimension to your life by becoming more acquainted with ferns. Your attitude toward your natural world will be greatly improved as will your sense of wonder. Ferns are spectacular plants but, please, don't fiddle around eating them!

Night Wings

Mention the word moth to some people and the first thing that comes to mind is clothes moths. All too frequently this accounts for the beginning and the end of their interest in these fascinating creatures. For sure the so-called Tineid (TIN-ee-id) Moths, comprising around 125 North American species, inflict plenty of damage to improperly stored woolen fabrics, feathers, fur and other animal products, but they are greatly outnumbered by thousands of intriguing, beautiful and useful species.

Notice the narrow antennae of this female Luna Moth. Those of the male are about twice as wide. Picture in your mind a light green jade color. Now imagine the incredible beauty of this large nighttime creature slowly flying by. My prediction is that few insects in flight will move you as much as that of the Luna Moth.

Our observations made while driving at night during the past few weeks have led us to believe that the large silk moths, seen either in the headlight beams of our car or fluttering near highway lights at road intersections, are more numerous than in previous years. Included in this group of our largest moths are the Luna, Cecropia, Polyphemus and Promethea. Needless to say, I immediately slow down my car as soon as I become aware of a flight of these awesome insects.

Other big night-flying moths, not quite as large in their wingspan as the giant silk moths, are the sphinx moths. A fairly common species in this region is the Five-spotted Hawkmoth whose wingspan can reach four and a half inches. Many of you may not be familiar with the adult moth but surely you know its larva, the Tomato Hornworm.

We have accidentally left our outside front door light on a few times during the month of July in past years and were invariably rewarded the following morning with a marvelous show of moths of various sizes clinging to the siding of our house. Our favorite has been the Luna with its white abdomen and pale jade-green wings with long, sweeping, extended "tail" tips. Each of the four wings sports a transparent spot. The leading edges of its forewings are a deep violet color.

Its rather slow loping flight is downright spectacular, exactly what you would expect from such a huge, heavy-bodied creature having such delicate wings. There is only one species in the *Actias* genus (AK-tee-us) in temperature North America. There are other species in the Old World. Fortunately the Luna Moth has an extensive range from Canada to Florida, westward to Texas and into the Great Plains.

Their larvae depend upon the leaves of some common trees including maples, alders, beeches, cherries, hazelnuts and willows. Cocoons are thin and papery and are spun among the leaves in the trees. Along with the leaves the cocoons fall to the ground in autumn and lie beneath the snow during the winter in this area.

Surprisingly the male Luna is capable of locating a female that is over a mile away. She emits a powerful odor (perfume to the male?) that is detected by the extremely perceptive sensory cells located on the male's antennae. By the way, the male's antennae are considerably wider than those of the female. The same holds true for many other moths. Butterflies lack this type of antenna and instead have thin, wiry, knob-tipped "feelers."

The male and female Lunas will unite, sperm is transferred, and the male then takes off in search of another female. Nature has provided the female Luna, as well as other moth species, with a little sac called the spermatheca which is directly attached to her reproductive system. Following mating, the male's sperm cells are stored in this container. In other words the eggs are not fertilized immediately upon the mating of the moths. Life span of these Luna moths, at most, is about two weeks. They and other giant silk moths have no mouth parts and, consequently, are incapable of feeding. Their only function in life is to reproduce their own kind.

Not all moths are night fliers. In fact one of our favorites is the Eight-spotted Forester, a tiny black moth having two very pale yellow spots on each of its two forewings and two white spots on each of its two hindwings. What a flashy little insect. Its wingspan is a little over one inch. The host food of its larvae are the leaves of grapes and Virginia Creepers.

Now that the flower gardens are beginning to do so well you can expect to see some of the other day-flying moths that resemble hummingbirds. In fact one species is called the hummingbird moth in light of its rather close resemblance to these "hovering" birds. Actually a better name is the Clearwing Hummingbird Moth in that all of its four wings have sizable glass-like transparent areas.

Those of you who garden and know all about cabbage loopers may be surprised to learn that these are the larvae (caterpillars, not worms!) of one of the hundreds of species of intricately marked Geometer (gee-OM-e-ter) Moths. Another common name for the caterpillar is inchworm.

I have mentioned enjoying seeing the hawkmoths ahead of the car headlights at night. Actually there are many species, most of which are known for their fast flight, up to about 30 MPH or more. Even though they are made like a biplane they fly like a monoplane.

Fastened to the front edge of the posterior wings of these and many other moths is a group of bristles called the frenulum (FREN-you-lum), nature's velcro. These bristles interlock with a unique process into the front wings thereby uniting the wings during flight. Butterflies lack the frenulum.

Even though moths outnumber butterflies about fourteen to one they are understood and appreciated by the average person far less than their colorful day-flying relatives. Borrow from your library or purchase a good book about moths, such as *Butterflies and Moths,* one of the Golden Nature Guides, or *Eastern Moths,* a Peterson Field Guide. They will help to satisfy your curiosity, increase your awareness of nature and help you to realize what great beauty in moths alone can be found in your own backyard!

July

Playing Possum

The extremes to which many wild creatures go in order to protect themselves or their young is quite wonderful. Take for example the time I was leading a group of people down a trail where some tall Brome Grass had bent over, concealing the narrow path. Suddenly a Woodcock fluttered up within four feet of where I was about to step. Its flight was slow and its actions different than other woodcocks I had seen fly.

Instinctively I looked downward and there, huddled next to the edge of the path, were three tiny Woodcock chicks. They hugged the ground and pulled in their necks for all they were worth. Quickly I instructed my group to stay to the extreme right of the trail and to carefully scrutinize every little patch of ground they would step upon. My immediate concern was for the adult mother bird to return to her brood as quickly as possible.

Later we marveled at the chicks' obedience and the mysterious manner in which the parent had communicated with her offspring telling them to "stay put!"

Several years ago we had a similar experience. In that instance the female Woodcock gave her low cackling distress call as she continued to run excitedly in about a 50-foot circle around us.

For once in my life I had a camera hanging around my neck when I needed it. Hearing some rustling in the dried leaves I stepped around the east side of our house and discovered a surprised and "cornered" Opossum that had no direct line of escape. Several pictures later, off it ambled into the nearby woods where it very likely hid under one of several protective brush piles. Note the long sensory hairs decorating its snout.

The young had just hatched and were still in the nest. They never flinched a muscle or a pin feather during the 30 seconds we observed them.

Killdeer parents, conspicuous birds of the open, strikingly marked, restless "loudmouths," are famous for their broken wing act. This lure display, injury feigning or whatever you wish to call it, does attract attention thereby enticing people or other potential predators away from the eggs or babies.

Some bird behaviorists believe that the floundering crippled display occurs as a result of the adult bird's inability to act simultaneously to two overpowering drives. One is to flee the nest and attack the predator. The other is to remain at the nest and staunchly defend the eggs or young.

The scientists refer to this ritual as a distraction display and place the emphasis on its demonstrated effectiveness rather than on the assumed purpose of the bird's actions. I tend to prefer the less scientific explanation and will always respond to a "suffering" adult Killdeer as it works in desperation with frenzied wing and tail movements in order to lead me away from its most prized and only possession.

Occasionally a photograph, in this case the Killdeer in distress, reveals another dimension to the total stratagem. The placement of the Killdeer's eyes is such that it can actually see behind its back. The bird has spread its beautiful tail to reveal the light, eye-catching cinnamon colored rump patch, the flashy white and black outer tail feathers, as well as the white tail feather tips. It flops and flutters hopelessly "injured" along the ground, but even though the bird moves directly away from you, nature has provided it with such fantastic vision that it can keep watch of every move you make.

Field observers have discovered that invariably a Killdeer will fly toward a person, then feign injury and attempt to lead you away as you approach its nest. However, should the intruder be a horse or cow, the bird will fly up into the face of the interloper until it turns away.

One of the most unbelievable distraction displays I have ever seen performed was that of a Hog-nosed Snake. A group of Madison Boy Scouts and I were exploring an alluring little creek out in the countryside one weekend when we discovered the snake next to an old tumble-down bridge. Just by coincidence we had cornered the three-foot reptile against the concrete abutment cutting off its chances of escape.

Immediately the snake extended and flattened its head and neck and made violent hissing noises as it lunged at us repeatedly. This mock ferocity persisted until the snake obviously sensed its futility. Now it began to tightly coil its body and to writhe and twist with great energy. Next it opened its mouth while the mouth and tongue appeared to ooze blood. Squirming, twining, and bleeding, the snake appeared as though it was dying an agonizing death.

Little by little the snake relaxed, turned its belly upward and lay motionless. We lifted the lifeless form without it revealing any signs of consciousness. As quickly as we turned the snake back onto its belly it immediately rolled over onto its back. Finally we retreated a short distance and sat down to watch for any changes in the Hog-nosed Snake's condition. Ever so slowly its head was raised. Sensing that all danger was out of sight the snake quickly regained normality and slithered away to safety.

Another classic example of protection from predators is that of the slow-moving common Opossum. This quiet, sleepy, solitary creature will fool you with its unusual durability and vitality. Hopelessly cornered, it will fall into a coma, body limp, eyes closed, and finally produce that famous cynical "grin" or silly-appearing "smile" by baring its upper teeth. Experts believe that this wonderful acting is brought about by a nervous reaction and is not intentional.

We pity the lowly small-brained Opossum yet note with deep satisfaction the hundreds of other creatures that protect the lives of their young as well as their own by "playing possum!"

A Honey Of A Tree

Have you heard of the "dances" of honey bees in their hives, signaling amounts of nectar to be had and in which direction it is to be found? Well, these vital little insects, even though they are not native to this country, must be dancing now as they've not done in a few years.

Walk into a typical eastern Wisconsin woods at this season, enjoy the quiet atmosphere, the lazy warmth, the peaceful "churk—churk—churk" of a Chipmunk in the distance – and suddenly notice an indescribably pleasant, gentle perfume flowing into your nostrils.

From overhead comes a steady, soft humming sound signaling without words or voice the type of tree under which you are standing – a Basswood. If you have European background you may wish to call it a Linden tree. Bees have been attracted from a considerable distance to the ambrosial nectar of these huge flowering "towers."

Tens of thousands of half-inch-long, creamy-white to yellowish flowers hang in small cymes (pronounced 'simes'), broad, flattish inflorescences borne on stout stalks. Each flower cluster emanates from a long leaf-like bract which, when the small, hard, furry nutlets ripen and fall, will parachute them downward and away from the parent tree where their likelihood of germinating will increase.

The unusual late-forming flowers, loaded with sweet nectar, are somewhat mealy, easy to chew and surprisingly good. Connoisseurs of teas that are made from wild plants claim that Basswood tea is a delicacy. Fresh flowers are dried indoors at room temperature. A teaspoon of flowers steeped in boiled water is said to produce a tea described as soft, well flavored and sweet.

Study the life of this unusually fine tree and you'll be amazed at its importance to people throughout history. Native Americans of this region made excellent binding material and ropes

If you enjoy the flavor of Basswood honey you'll undoubtedly relish the delicate taste of tea brewed from the dried flowers of this widespread tree. After the flowers have been dried indoors at room temperatures for several days they are ready for use. One teaspoon per cup of boiling water should do the trick – and have you asking for more.

from the tree's inner bark which has incredibly long and tough fibers. This so-call "bast" led to its common name of Bastwood, which quite naturally through the years was unwittingly corrupted to Basswood.

The rope was said to be softer, easier on the hands and equally as tough as some of the modern ropes made from jute and other natural fibers. Asian relatives to our Basswood tree are used to produce jute which in turn is made into ropes, burlap material and gunnysacks.

The wood of these large imposing trees, known in past years as "show trees of the great," is considered to be a soft hardwood having straight grain and fine uniform texture. Generally it is described as a featureless wood. Stain the wood properly and it compares quite favorably with Black Walnut.

A host of products have been made through the years from this wood, including drawer sides, window frames, musical instruments, piano keys and occasionally sounding boards, high-quality picture puzzles, venetian blinds and drawing boards. Because the light-colored wood is free from taint, it has been widely used for making frames for beehives and comb honey, berry boxes, butter tubs and crates and boxes for cheese.

If you can think back to the olden days of excelsior, used in packing prior to the invention of the abominable plastic pellets, the excelsior, too, was made largely from Basswood. (Bear in mind that wood comes from trees, a renewable resource, whereas plastic in general is derived from a non-renewable resource, oil!)

Many of the best woodcarvers and whittlers in the business use Basswood lumber. Not only can Basswood be carved well (with sharp blades!) but it also takes paints and stains nicely.

Years ago there was great hope in Europe that an excellent substitute for chocolate could be derived from the fruits and flowers of Basswood, furnishing a paste that in texture and taste closely resembled chocolate. Unfortunately it did not store well and decomposed rather quickly. According to the literature, all of these attempts involved the use of European species of Linden or so-called "Lime" trees, the same genus but different species than our Basswood. Perhaps attempts should be made in this country using American species, of which several exist.

There are some foresters and nursery workers who believe a Basswood's vices outweigh its virtues. Quite a few of these trees send up numerous sucker shoots, the shapes of some specimens become quite gangly and wild, and the high sugar content of its leaves and flowers attracts huge quantities of aphids.

One of the most famous avenues in the world, *Unter den Linden* in Berlin, Germany, is lined with Lindens as is the avenue at Trinity College in Cambridge, England.

Count yourselves lucky if somehow you can enjoy the beauty, cool shade, fragrant flowers, imposing tower-like stature, lovely winter silhouette and other fine features a "Bastwood" has to offer during the cycle of a year. We strongly concur with the bees. Here is a honey of a tree!

Flowers' Gentle Partners

A few summers ago Charlotte and I were guests in the late afternoon at an exceptionally wonderful backyard concert presented by two professional lady musicians. One sang and the other played the Celtic harp. It was on a small natural stage between two large yellow-flowering Shrubby Potentilla bushes that the women performed.

Unknown to the Celtic harp player and singer, and very likely to most of the small audience, a tiny Dorcas Copper butterfly continuously flitted back and forth between the two Potentilla shrubs while the ladies thrilled the audience with their performance of the musical selections. It so happens that the Shrubby Potentilla is the host plant to this little-understood butterfly. The rather soft ethereal music matched to perfection the noiseless flight of the butterfly. This was the first time, and perhaps the last, that I witnessed the flight of a butterfly accompanied by music.

There is little doubt in my mind that the most commonly seen butterfly species in this part of the state thus far this summer has been the tiny Pearl Crescent Spot, common from Canada to Mexico. In fact it is a genus found from southern Argentina north to the Mackenzie River on the Arctic Ocean. You will frequently see them visiting flowers and the edges of puddles.

Their wingspan is about one and one-quarter inches. They often alight, hold their wings outward, then pump them up and down a few times warming their bodies almost motionlessly in the sun. Occasionally they will fan their wings back and forth. Males have more orange on the upper wing surfaces while females have more brown. I have frequently seen them sunning on Black-eyed Susan wildflowers that are so abundant throughout the countryside in July.

Another butterfly species that is very common during this season is the Eyed Brown. They have a wingspan of about two inches and are light brown or tan to dark brown and have a series of tiny dark colored eyespots surrounded by light yellow near the margins of their wings. They belong to a group called the Satyrs which for this region may also include the Pearly Eye and the Little Wood Satyr.

If you think Michael Jordan, the basketball great, has a lot of cool moves, you should try, using a butterfly net, to catch a Little Wood Satyr or an Eyed Brown. You're in for quite a surprise. Outwardly they appear rather slow — until you begin chasing them. Now they suddenly twist, feint, bob and weave their way through the grasses and shrubs showing you some of the most skillful dodging moves you've ever seen. Jordan couldn't hold a candle to their skills in resisting capture.

A small orange and dark brown butterfly, Milbert's Tortoise-shell, having black-edged wings decorated with blue spots on the hind wings and orange dashes on the forewings, has become one of my favorites. It is never abundant. An interesting experiment was done with a close relative,

The size of this Northern Pearly Eye Butterfly, handsomely marked with eyespots, can be more accurately judged when you realize that this one is drinking the juice of an orange cut in half. Note its uncoiled proboscis (pro-BOS-sis) curved downward to reach the orange. Apparently the color of the orange is what initially attracted the butterfly. However, it was the bottom of its feet through which it tasted the sweet flesh of the fruit.

the Small Tortoise Shell butterfly, whereby a record was kept of the number of visits these butterflies made to various white, pink and purple flowers. Of over 425 visits recorded, these butterflies made more than half of their visits to purple flowers. Next came pink while fewer than 50 visits were made to white flowers.

The first large blossoms have appeared on the Purple Coneflowers in our butterfly garden. Hopefully one of these days we will enjoy several different butterfly species visiting these or other pink to purple flowers growing there. The pink-flowering Buddleia, often called Butterfly Bush, attracted many butterflies last summer.

One of the larger, more conspicuous butterflies of this region, the Mourning Cloak, has been noticeably down in number this summer. I am inclined to think that the extremely cold weather of the winter before last was very hard on their population in that this species overwinters as adults. Thousands may have frozen to death. They simply crawl into a woodpile in late fall or force their way under a loose piece of bark on a tree and winter there. Come the first spring warmth they are out and about.

Their wingspan can be slightly over three inches. The dark purplish-brown wings are edged with creamy yellow, and just inside these yellow bands are single rows of light blue dots. Their larvae feed on any of the many species of willow shrubs and trees. I've fairly regularly seen a small number throughout the summer and hopefully their population will have recovered by next year. This favorite butterfly numbers among several others that have landed on our hands or arms and remained there for considerable periods feasting on the salts and other minerals contained in our body perspiration.

It has been said that butterflies are the only "bugs" that people aren't afraid of. They can't bite or sting and they won't chase after you. They go wherever they please and they please wherever they go. The fact that these insects (No, they are not bugs!) are primarily day fliers, especially on sun-drenched days, and are attracted to colorful flower beds should make flower gardening doubly pleasant for people to enjoy.

A much-talked-about phenomenon this summer (1995) involves the Monarch butterfly. So many friends have asked why there are so few of these large, widely known and admired butterflies in the region. How I wish that Susan Borkin or Dr. Allen Young of the Milwaukee Public Museum could more appropriately answer this question.

I have heard that logging operations on the lower slopes of the pine-clad mountains of central Mexico, where the Monarch butterflies from our part of the country winter, have ruthlessly overcut the forests there and are dangerously affecting the required conditions for proper wintering on the part of these creatures. The total we have seen on our property this entire summer has been two! Many people have seen a total of zero! (Their numbers had rebounded by the summer of 1999, and most Door Countyites were enjoying the best Monarch year in a long time.)

Apparently when Dr. Lincoln Brower, the Monarch butterfly expert of the world, predicted in a speech we heard him present several years ago that conceivably we would see the end of the Monarch butterfly migration in central and eastern United States within a 20-year period he knew what he was talking about! How tragic!

Ecosystems gradually deteriorate at the hands of people and, finally, years later with tiny remaining fragments of the original plants, animals and insects still intact, the biologists are coaxed into trying vainly to bring back the beauty of the natural plants and animals. Knowing what is occurring rampantly around the world you'd think the logical direction to be taking NOW is to learn what our immediate environments are like, precisely what they contain, the elements and balances required to maintain the various healthy viable components — and to keep them that way. Unfortunately money speaks much louder than do butterflies — and people who like them.

Snakes Alive!

One of the happiest days of my early boyhood was the last day I was a third grader, even though a part of the memorable experience backfired. Our teacher, Florence Zuell, chose to take us on our class picnic out to the dam along the Kewaunee River, the site of an old feed mill that at one time was powered by a waterwheel. The mill had been torn down and the dam was in some-what of a state of ruin, but what a perfect place for young, curious naturalists to explore. Inter-estingly my Great-grandfather Skala was the miller at that mill for many years.

We had finished our picnic lunch and were free "within bounds" to make our fun on this much-waited-for day. Several of us boys soon discovered some Grass Snakes (as we called them) living in a tumbled-down stone wall. This was the day, the first time in my life, that I learned that Grass Snakes (which really were Smooth Green Snakes, bright green above and white or yellow-ish-white below) were easy to catch, were very smooth and dry to the touch, didn't struggle or attempt to bite you, and were fascinating to look at.

I was so enraptured and triumphant over this new experience that some inner force moved me to want to share this joy with Roxi Lichterman, the lady who had given several other students and me a ride to the dam. She was sitting some distance away in their new 1938 Buick. The window was rolled down and she was reading as I ran excitedly up to the car. Without thinking I shouted, "Roxi, look what I found!" and thrust the gorgeous smooth green creature in to show her. One look at the snake and she screamed bloody murder! Then when she regained her composure she yelled at the top of her voice, "Get that snake out of here!"

That triggered a quick response from Miss Zuell, and in about 10 seconds my overwhelming feeling of mastery over the snake was shattered. Instead of a rewarding experience, the Smooth

Even though the Eastern Garter Snake is non-venomous, along with all the rest of the wild snakes of northeastern Wisconsin, it is one you may not wish to handle. At least you may wish you hadn't handled it once you held it in our hands and then released it. Most will have ejected a very smelly musk from scent glands that are located near the base of the tail.

Green Snake expedition turned into one of reprimand and shame. But deep down I was happy.
Never again would I be terrified by snakes, but rather tolerant and understanding of these useful
reptiles.

Many snake experiences through the years, coupled with study about them, have taught me
that there are no records of venomous snakes in northeastern Wisconsin. The "Water Moccasin
Snakes" killed and brought to me in the past for identification all turned out to be dark brown
Northern Water Snakes. True, they can be quite cantankerous. In fact their fierce objection to
your interruption of their privacy might lead you to believe they would rather fight than do
anything else. They are considered to be second in abundance in the state to Eastern Garter
Snakes.

Without a doubt the most incorrectly identified snake in this region is the Western Fox Snake.
Almost everyone calls it the Pine Snake and many insist that they are Copperheads and must be
done away with. True Pine Snakes are southern and eastern snakes. The light tan to reddish-tan
head prompts people to fear and kill it. Their hasty unfounded reasoning is that they have done
the world a favor by killing a venomous snake when in fact they have taken the life of the best
"mouser" on their property.

A small group of us on an exploratory outing a few years ago came upon an adult Fox Snake,
about 50 inches long, sunning on the low half-rotted roof of a small machine shed on an aban-
doned farm. What surprised us was the loud nervous rattling noise it made with its tail as it
vibrated against the old dry cedar shingles. Several of these snakes on a farm can be considered
extremely valuable because of their fondness of rodents. They will never chase you, but rather do
their utmost to hide from you.

The only snake one might confuse with the Fox Snake in this area is the less common Milk
Snake. Their color markings can be fairly similar. The very easiest way to identify the Milk
Snake is by the whitish Y-shaped marking on the top of its head. Another way to positively

identify each, should the spirit move you, is to capture them and examine their anal scales. The Fox Snake has a divided anal scale whereas the Milk Snake has a single anal scale.

Every one of about a dozen snake skins I've found in the wood pile in the past few years has turned out to be that of the Eastern Garter Snake, sleek striped reptile. They shed their skins two or three times a year. When this snake is ready to shed its skin, its eyes are a hazy bluish-gray. They will be a bright shiny black once the skin has been shed. Examine the cast-off skin and you will be surprised to find that it covers the snake's eyes too, like miniature contact lenses.

Snakes are about as popular with a majority of people as are spiders, and for this reason relatively little is known or cared about these beneficial animals. My field experiences in northeastern Wisconsin have turned up the following (all non-venomous and harmless): Western Fox, Eastern Milk, Northern Water, DeKay's or Brown, Northern Red-bellied, Eastern Garter, Smooth Green and Northern Ring-necked. The following two species, which I have seen elsewhere in the state, should also exist in this region: the Bull Snake and the Hog-nosed Snake.

The Bull Snake is the largest of Wisconsin snakes, often attaining a length of up to eight feet. This rodent-destroyer, with its great size, loud hiss and tail-vibrating habits, will scare some people half out of their shoes. I am still looking for my first one in this part of the state.

The total value of every one of our native snakes cannot be overestimated. Little is known about their status, a fact directly related to people's lack of good sound education through the years. Help the total environmental picture by learning all you can about these important creatures. Share your knowledge with others. The first step and responsibility we have in helping our ailing Earth is to learn about all of its inhabitants, snakes included. Consider yourself a partner in nature.

It invariably is during summer droughts that birdbaths become incredibly important and heavily visited. Add a simple device to provide constant dripping of water into your baths, placed upon the ground, and their effectiveness and attractiveness to the birds will increase greatly. Ours are scrubbed out with an old broom several times a day and replenished with clean water when they are being used a lot. The largest bird we have ever observed at one of our baths was a young Northern Goshawk whose total body length was greater than the diameter of the garbage can cover!

Water Your Birds!

Someone recently asked me, "When do you suggest I begin to feed the birds?" My answer, without hesitation, was, "Today!" I know it was a curt answer, but it expressed my sincerity. In a way it was like my Dad's answer to one of his customers at the barbershop years ago who asked him, "Adolph, how should I prune the apple trees in my backyard?" My Dad's answer – "Six inches from the ground!"

His answer reflected genuine experiences. He had always maintained that unless all of one's neighbors spray and carefully tend their trees too, you can't expect to have anything but wormy apples. His advice was to buy one's apples from a good apple-grower who is an expert in the business.

Likewise you can't expect to have birds nearby if food is unavailable, natural or otherwise. And if you wish to have more birds to watch and enjoy in summer too, then continue your feeding program. As a matter of fact, why stop at all? I would like to see proof that a bird, eating your handouts day after day, can't find its own wild food too. Personally I believe that most birds liberally supplement your handouts with plenty of natural food. Remember that once you begin feeding birds you cannot stop abruptly without creating hardships or even casualties.

Another frequently overlooked requirement of birds, of great importance in most summers, is water. Practically every good book dealing with attracting birds to your yard includes providing them with food, water, shelter, nesting sites, and protection from unnatural enemies, such as feral cats.

Consider the physiology of birds. This will help you to develop a better understanding of their need for water. Birds don't perspire. Instead, blood vessels in their skins expand slightly on warmer days helping to release heat, and the birds' rate of breathing increases. Water evaporates from their respiratory channels. I am sure you have watched the little puffs of condensed water vapor coming from their mouths as the birds perched on your feeders on sub-zero days.

They require much less water relative to their weight than many other animals. Those living in arid parts of the world are conditioned to requiring less water and to being the most active during the coolest hours of daylight.

You may have seen birds, such as Black-capped Chickadees, eating snow in order to get water. This precious substance, water, is not only obtained by drinking but also through food that is eaten. Included are insects, earthworms, foliage containing a lot of water, or even dew found on plants in the early morning.

Consider the problem that certain migratory birds, such as gulls, terns and ducks, must face. Many live in northern, inland, freshwater regions during the summer, then migrate to coastal saltwater areas for the winter. How can they survive by drinking the same salty water that would kill a human being? They're equipped with nasal glands, located on top of their head between their eyes, capable of absorbing and excreting nearly all of the salt taken in.

Experience has taught us several things about birds and their need of water. Birds tend to prefer to bathe in shallow pools on the ground. Unfortunately this makes them vulnerable to the feral cats on the loose. You will also have to figure out ways of keeping these unwelcome predators away from your feeding areas.

Birds dislike slippery surfaces, such as smooth plastic. I salvaged an old washing machine cover from the dump many years ago. It was made of rough-textured aluminum and became the birds' favorite bath and drinking fountain. Add a source of falling water to the ground-level bath and this "dripping magic" will lure birds and other small creatures to the "watering hole" which otherwise would seldom appear. Some of our favorites in recent years have been the Brown Thrasher, Wood Thrush, Scarlet Tanager and Ovenbird.

Dripping water can be provided by a hose and fine nozzle suspended a foot or more above the bath. A simpler and less expensive way is to punch a nail through the bottom of a large tin can which then is suspended a few feet directly above the bath. Make the hole from the inside, then leave the nail in the hole to provide a slow, irresistible tinkling dribble of welcome water. A plastic gallon milk jug, with a small hole punched along the side, slightly above the bottom, also works quite well as an inexpensive water dripper.

The closer to trees and shrubs your birdbath is the better the birds will like it. A White-throated Sparrow, who absolutely dominated the bath, dunked itself, followed by the usual vigorous feather shaking, over 30 times in a row one day. He flew (barely) to the lowest overhead branch where he completed his bathing ritual that included much feather rearranging and preening.

Experts have been stumped as to why birds bathe. It could be they are no different than many people who like to occasionally splash around in the water. Others say they do it to cool their bodies. Do you suppose that birds bathe in order to become cleaner? It has been said that birds bathe in winter to clean their plumage which, in turn, will then keep their bodies warmer when many of the feathers are fluffed outward. There are also some who contend that birds dunk themselves into the water to get rid of parasites.

Personally I favor the cleanliness idea. Our good friend, Miss Emma Toft, contended that if people would use soap, water and a brush they wouldn't have to use perfume. All they would have to add is a nice smile to be truly beautiful. And if the birds don't smile in approval, at least we do at their apparent joy and antics as they stand, splashing, belly-deep in the water of the old washing machine cover.

August

Phantom Of The Woods

Ideal growing conditions have triggered the appearance of many isolated little clusters of one of nature's most unusual plants. Few wildflowers are as fungus-like, bleached and immaculate as the Indian Pipe. In fact they look downright supernatural – regular little phantoms of the deep shaded woods.

It is difficult to imagine that a seed-producing flower can be colorless. A mass of brittle, white, fiber-like roots obtain this mystic plant's food mostly from decomposing vegetable matter. This qualifies it to be classed as a saprophyte, which in Greek means "rotten plant." It also derives a small amount of its nourishment from living roots giving it parasitic tendencies as well.

People with vivid imaginations have nicknamed the Indian Pipe the ice plant, corpse plant, Dutchman's Pipe and fairy smoke. Its generic name, *Monotropa,* means one turn. At an early stage of its development the flowering stem is turned slightly to one side. Also the plant turns straight upward as the seeds ripen and remains in that position throughout the winter. The species name, *uniflora*, tells us it is a one-flowered plant. Each clammy white blossom grows from a scape, a naked flowering stem arising from the ground.

It is not uncommon for people to gasp in surprise at their first sight of flowering Indian Pipes, so unusually beautiful and mysterious are they. Get down upon the ground for a close look and, when the light is just right, you may detect a very delicate pink color on some of the plants. A small silvered reflector was used to capture a ray of sunshine hitting the ground about 10 feet behind the plants, then reflected onto the backsides of the Indian Pipes providing them with subtle backlighting for this photograph taken through a 105 mm macro lens.

These weirdly beautiful herbs thrive among decayed leaves and appear to survive best in heavily-shaded, moist, rich woods especially under pine and oak trees. They can be found almost throughout temperate North America. Our wildflower calendar indicates they appear in this area usually during mid to late July and into early August.

Each pallid, narrow, cup-shaped blossom has four, five or occasionally six petals. The only leaves are mere scales or bracts, few in number, situated along the stem. They are very delicate, fine-toothed and paper-thin.

The flower hangs from its bent stalk like a bowed head until nearly ripe. Slowly the blossom turns upward as though wanting to say something. Now a delicately-colored portion of its reproductive parts is displayed to the insect world. Eight to 10 tiny yellow-tipped stamens can be seen.

All during its growth, from seed to its flowering stage, the Indian Pipe, lacking chlorophyll, has been unable to make its own food as nearly all other seed plants do. Instead it has to depend upon other living or non-living plants for all of its strength. Finally it has lifted its head straight upward toward the sky as though proudly shouting to the whole world, "Well, at least I can produce my own seeds!"

The stiff upright plants gradually turn black and will easily persist throughout winter. In fact it is common to see the remains of small clusters of last year's plants, about four to eight inches tall, next to the new ghostly scapes.

Occasionally a few of the delicate waxy plants, backlighted by the early morning sun, will reveal a beautiful pearly pink translucence. How smooth! How fragile and pale they are! Rarely will your hikes through the woods reward you as wonderfully and surprisingly as when you discover these tender little plants that surely possess virtuous charms, the Indian Pipes, phantoms of the woods.

Lacy Umbrellas

The world's experts in the manufacture of lace may reside in Belgium or Italy but the queen of the lace-maker's art graces practically every road side, waste place and dry field in eastern United States each August. A queen's title was too good for many farmers who lowered the name to wild carrot, bird's nest weed, or the devil's plague.

I sat at the kitchen table early this morning, the warm sunlight streaming over my shoulder, and thoroughly examined and admired a four-inch Queen Anne's Lace flower. One of my conclusions was that this intricate umbrella-shaped blossom was equally beautiful when viewed from the underside.

It belongs to the parsley, or better yet, the Umbelliferae (um-bel-LIF-er-ee) family. Umbrella family would suit me just fine! There are 45 genera in this interesting group, some edible including Caraway and Parsley, others deadly toxic, such as Poison Hemlock, the plant poison that killed Socrates. One of my favorites in the family is the Cow Parsnip, a towering plant of moist places.

I painstakingly dissected the entire flower head. Eight sepals composed of green, divided, thread-like bracts curved down and outward in a circular fashion beneath the umbel. Fifty-three separate floral clusters made up the entire head. Those located on the outer margin had the longest stalks. The large outer floral cluster I examined more closely contained 49 separate florets. Those along the outside edge had the largest white petals. A big Queen Anne's Lace flower might have as many as 2500 florets!

Fortunately the blossom I picked in the ditch had a single almost blackish-purple central floret. It was standing on its own tiny stalk. Some experts have come to believe that nature

This *Queen Anne's Lace* wildflower has sitting on top of it a *Flower Spider*, also referred to as a *Crab Spider*. Invariably the spider, which in this case is white with pink stripes near the sides of its abdomen, will be poised and facing the dark maroon "decoy flower" near the middle of the blossom. This tiny decoy flower presumably attracts insects to it which, in turn, will be preyed upon by the Crab Spider.

provided the "Queen" with this outstanding little target to serve as a decoy. The thought is that it resembles an insect and will therefore lure others to the flower, thereby helping to bring about cross-pollination.   Not all of the flowers have this central, dark-colored floret.

Old-timers with a more fluid imagination envisioned Queen Anne fastening her lace medallions upon her royal person with garnet-headed pins. Still others fancied the young queen pricking her finger with a needle while making lace and staining the center of her pattern with a single drop of blood!

This elegant nuisance of a plant was named *Daucus Carota* (DAW-cus ca-ROE-ta) by Linnaeus and literally means red-rooted umbelliferous plant. It is thought to be a wild form of a cultivated carrot that escaped from gardens many years ago, perhaps in the Netherlands region. It obviously became well-adapted to growing in the wild. In fact it ranges over three continents and continues to march westward in this country as its "empire" grows.

Much of its success can be traced to the simple fact that it is a biennial capable of producing nearly 7000 to 8000 seeds per large plant of nine or 10 flower heads. The seeds very likely germinate in late summer and fall. The next year a small rosette of feathery carrot-like leaves and a rather long, thin, fleshy root develop. This strong starchy taproot easily survives the winter.

A branching flower stalk, hollow, ridged and bristly, up to three or even more feet tall, develops during the second year. Several flat-topped lacy umbels adorn the plant. Larger showy white petals, situated around the border of the umbel, most likely help to attract insects. Less conspicuous hermaphrodite blossoms are clustered next to the showy ones. The entire central portion of the handsome circular arrangement consists of miniature pollen-bearing florets.

The outside seed-bearing stalks curve inward sharply as the flower ages and its fruits mature. Finally it becomes a "tight-fisted" cup-shaped cluster of stalks and seeds and somewhat resembles a bird's nest. These dry flower clusters frequently break off during winter storms and are blown over the crusty snow, merrily scattering hundreds of seeds along the way.

The garden carrot of today has evolved from many years of horticultural improvement. Chances are it has been improved so much that few species would winter here and produce seeds the second year. Not so with the dainty but durable wild carrot. Come mid-summer our roadsides and old fields are laced far and wide with those of Queen Anne herself, drop of blood included.

The Voiceless Singer

We boys, in our pre-teen-age years, were self-appointed prognosticators of the first magnitude. The most subtle sights or sounds prepared us for all sorts of things that were "bound" to happen.

One sound of mid-August caused us to suddenly take stock of our dwindling summer vacation—"freedom" we called it. The high, far-reaching, monotonous whining of the Cicadas meant that our days of carefree adventure would soon be over and it would be back to school. We had better speed up our pace of activity to complete all those "important" projects we had so carefully planned behind opened textbooks last May.

I could very likely include myself with thousands of others who for years have heard the lazy, droning, buzz-saw hum of the Cicadas, yet have seldom, if ever, seen one. How frustrating it had been to have to show people a picture of the sound-maker, that foretoken of late summer.

Finally, after more than a dozen years of interpreting nature for people, I found one. My group and I had been conscious of several of those "heard but not seen" creatures as we hiked

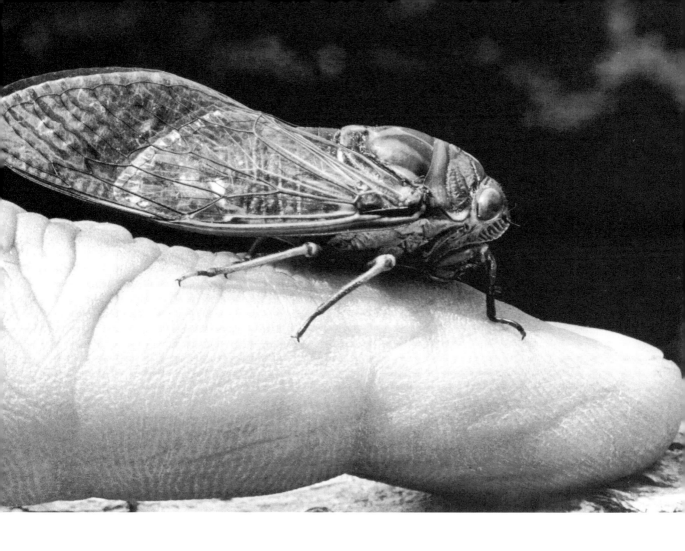

Even though Annual Cicadas such as this one photographed clinging to my index finger, lace the late summer air with their "love songs," they are never far from their predators. These may include American Kestrels, Blue Jays, House Sparrows, House Cats and Striped Skunks in our region. There remains the question of how long the larvae of the "Annual" Cicada, most widespread species in our region, remain underground. Estimates run to five years.

along the edge of the woods. Suddenly there one was, an inch-and-a-half long Cicada, clinging firmly to the bottom of a wooden trail sign.

How it buzzed in my cupped hands after I captured it. Slowly I released my grip on the large bug-eyed creature and it clung tightly to my finger. Now, finally, after all those years we could see, firsthand, what the ear-splitting instrumentalist looked like.

Instrumentalist is an appropriate title, at least for the male cicadas, because their sounds, like all other insects, are produced in one of various ways other than with true voices. Either they rub one part of their body against another, or, as is the case with the male Cicadas, the posterior part of their abdomen contains a pair of comparatively large drum heads where the sound is produced. High-pitched vibrations are made through the use of tympanal muscles, then provided with carrying power by resonators. Female Cicadas are voiceless.

Ancient Greeks considered Cicadas to be almost divine and frequently included them in their art, poetry and music. Their emblem depicting the science of music pictured a Cicada upon a harp. One Greek poet, possessed of a sense of humor, wrote, "Happy the Cicadas' lives, for they have voiceless wives."

One of the reasons why so few people ever see a Cicada is due to an interesting phase of their life cycle. The adult female lays eggs in slits cut into tree branches. The small nymphs hatch, fall to the ground and burrow in by using their strong front legs. They attach themselves to the roots of trees and, using their tubular mouths, withdraw liquid nourishment.

Some species of Cicadas may remain in the nymph stage underground for 17 to 20 years. Frequently, through error, one is called the 17-year Locust. It is a Cicada, not a Locust. The species of this region has a life cycle lasting about four years. Eventually a nymph will crawl out of the ground and onto the trunk or branch of a tree. The skin on the top of its head and upper abdomen splits, enabling the adult to emerge. Having beautiful glassy wings it can fly very well. The adults will mate, live for a few weeks and then die.

One experience I shall never forget occurred on my second day in the Army, back in late July of 1953. We left Milwaukee by bus on a searing hot day and arrived at Camp Crowder, Missouri late that night. By the time we had our first military "mess hall" meal and were issued bedding it was after midnight. I don't know if the Cicadas were the four-year, thirteen-year, or seventeen-year variety, and I didn't care. There were thousands of them out there in the dark, producing a din such as I had never heard before in my life. As my boyhood-developed prognostications told me, "Things could only get better!" I don't think any of us slept much that night.

Hopefully the day will arrive when you'll have the pleasure of being able to admire one of these unusual creatures from close range, "Mr. Late Summer," shiny transparent wings, short stout body, bulging eyes, built-in drum heads and producer of one of nature's most unforgettable August songs.

Spot The Amphibian

How little we know about frogs. Take for an example an experience a group of hikers and I had while walking along the western portion of Deerlick trail at the Ridges Sanctuary during the third week of August, 1970. Suddenly a very strange high-pitched squeal began no more than 25 feet away. None of us knew what was making the sound.

It turned out that a large Garter Snake had captured a medium-sized Leopard Frog in its jaws, hind feet first, causing the frog to call forth with its frenzied death scream. Later I learned that this is the only call herpetologists are aware of that frogs and toads make with their mouths open.

If I were to confront millions of suffering and dying amphibians, I surely couldn't be proud of my contribu-
tions to the air and water quality that may be harmfully affecting them. How do we better take care of wha
land and water we've got rather than being so smugly insulated and far removed from it? How can we
learn more from the natural world? Would it ever be possible for every American to carefully evaluate an
properly alter their lifestyle? Are we loving this earth to death?   The Native American, Chief Luther
Standing Bear, reached me with his poignant words: "Let us put our minds together to see what kind of
world we can make for our children."

I kneeled down just inches from the drama for a better look. The snake paid little attention to me until I gently nudged the frog's body. My first impulse had been to free the imprisoned frog from the grip of the snake, but my better judgment sided with the snake. They too need food, and here was ecology, natural selection, survival of the fittest, balance of nature, all unfolding vividly before our eyes.

The very second I touched the frog's body the snake's tail extended upward and quivered, absolutely vibrated in warning against the grasses and twigs. Then slowly it raised its head nearly a foot above the ground and retreated, quite majestic-like in its movements, with the frog into the higher vegetation.

Having begun working at the sanctuary in June of 1964, I observed what I thought were normal Leopard Frog populations for the following seven or eight years. Late August found the wet margins of the swales so abundant with these spotted frogs that one almost had to be careful to not step on them, or so it appeared.

How drastically the picture had changed by the summer of 1975. Prior to that year Green Frogs by the dozens had strummed their "loose-stringed banjos" in the swampy northern reaches of the Mud Lake Wildlife Area north of Baileys Harbor. Now we heard none, and we have heard none since then.

Leopard Frogs too, once so extremely abundant, had vanished as though by magic. Reports began to surface from throughout the United States and Canada. Reductions in their populations were astounding, 50 percent, 90 percent, and in some previously high-count areas not one Leopard Frog could be found.

Up to about 1963 a leading biological supply house in the Midwest had been shipping in excess of 30 tons of Leopard Frogs annually to high schools, colleges and scientific laboratories. Today that creature has virtually ceased being an animal used for experimentation.

Possible reasons for the frightening disappearance and reduction of so many species of frogs and toads worldwide have included loss of habitat, fragmentation of habitat, over-exploitation by people, spread of competing exotic species, human interference such as pollution, climate change, and the increase in UV-B radiation thereby weakening the frogs' and toads' immune systems. One biologist summed up the situation by stating simply that they are disappearing due to humans' insensitivity to the earth's environment.

The study of some frogs is a fascinating hands-on research project. Many are colorful creatures to photograph and to write about. When one or more species suddenly becomes threatened or endangered as to its very existence the public soon learns about it. Unfortunately such is not the case with the extinction of about 17,500 species of plants, animals and insects occurring annually as a direct result of the tropical forest destruction in Central and South America. One can only wonder in awe at how many species became extinct with the "slaughter" of the old-growth forests in North America before the turn of the century.

I nearly danced with joy in early August of 1999 when friends with Charlotte and me at Toft Point discovered a huge healthy-appearing Leopard Frog, one of the largest I've ever seen. Rather than the usual green color, this one was very bronzy and some of its irregular dark spots were faintly rimmed with green. What a gorgeous frog! Upon attempting to approach it for photographs it soon displayed its leaping ability — five or more feet!

I wish I had a nickel today for every Leopard Frog I tried to catch when I was a young, summer-vacationing school boy at home. On the other hand if I had been paid a quarter for every one I did capture, my piggy bank would have had very little jingle to it!

We caught frogs out of pure fun and never tried to make a science out of it. I finally learned that if you cautiously approach them at a right angle from the side and then make your lightning-swift move you stand a better chance of snaring these slippery creatures.

If you are lucky enough to capture one, or even get near a live specimen, look closely at its eyes. They are truly beautiful, having an orange-gold iris and black pupil. These frogs have a light line on their upper jaw and can easily be told from their relatives, the Pickerel Frogs. The Leopard's hind legs are white on the undersides while the Pickerel's are yellowish-orange.

The point that scares me is that when a species starts to decline in number it's usually too late to help them. Often times scientific study amounts to little else but writing an obituary for a species. The Leopard Frog, like the miner's canary in the cage, should be a trumpeting herald, a high-pitched, shrill warning to humans that it's high time we get shaken out of our passive unconcern over the steady deterioration of the environment, particularly the millions of tons and gallons of biocides (killers of life) this sick planet of ours is pelted with each year.

I dread the thought of the Leopard Frog becoming another Passenger Pigeon — extinct — forever! Yes, I challenge you to go out and catch a Leopard Frog. As a matter of fact consider yourself lucky to be able to find one!

Big Daddy Stiltwalker

It's difficult to imagine anyone being afraid of a perfectly harmless, inoffensive, slow-moving Daddy-long-legs. Call them Harvestmen, Harvesters, Grandfather Greybeards, Haymakers, or our favorite name, Daddy-long-legs, they are valuable creatures that help people considerably by consuming large numbers of insects. They are important cogs in the natural system of checks and balances.

Common names for spiders and their close relatives are both interesting and abundant. In fact, some references call the long-legged spider that spins loose webs in dark corners of houses or cellars and usually hangs upside down the Daddy-long-legs. You will also discover that some Daddy-long-legs have short legs and should more appropriately be called Daddy-short-legs!

If you wish to be technical, the Daddy-long-legs we know so well are not true spiders. They do not spin webs or leave behind a drag-line wherever they walk, as do the true spiders. They have no poisonous bite and their head, thorax and abdomen are all grown together as one unit. True spiders have distinct parts, the cephalothorax at the front to which the legs are attached, and the large abdomen toward the rear.

Spider or not, the "Big Daddy" deserves more respect and a closer look by everyone. I was amazed when I examined one of its legs for the first time. I found a dead specimen and chose one of its second pair for a detailed study. These are the longest, have sensitive tips and are used in exploring the surroundings. They're spread widely when the spider is running.

The first joint, the coxa, resembles a tiny socket and is firmly attached to the body. The second, the trochanter, is a tiny black knob and appears more ornamental than anything. The third segment is the femur similar to a person's thighbone. It is quite long, angled upward and gives the creature its stiltlike appearance.

A tiny, knobby "kneebone," the patella, makes up its fourth segment. The tibia, like your shinbone, is fairly long and usually quite parallel to the ground. The last two segments, the metatarsus and tarsus, appear as one and give this dawdling predator the long-legged look.

I marvel at how delicately the two longest legs, resembling inquisitive "feelers," can sweep the ground ahead as though reading the landscape for hidden danger. Actually, Daddy's eyes are also used for observation. What appears to be a very tiny, single eye resembling a minuscule wart located near the front of the body, contains two shiny black eyes. A ten-power lens is needed to see them well.

Situated between the jaws and front legs are two small chelicerae (ki-LISS-er-ee). They have tiny hooks or claws on the end and are used to transfer food to the mouth or to squash tiny insects so they can be sucked dry of body fluids.

It is quite common to see a Daddy-long-legs with a leg or two missing, perhaps resulting from a close encounter with one of its predators, a bird, for example. These missing appendages cannot

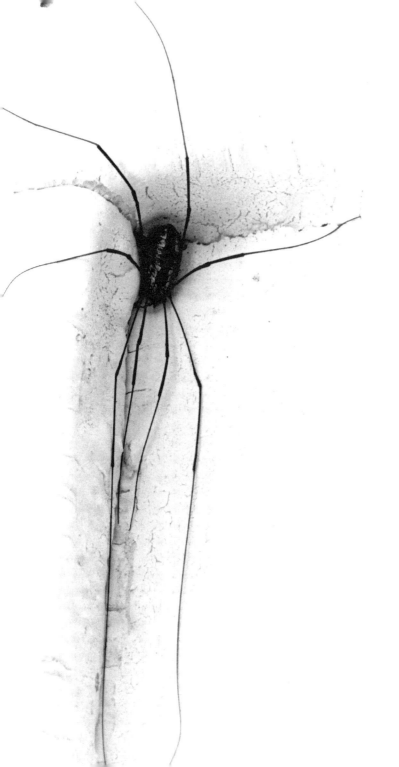

The eight-legged Daddy-long-legs belongs to that group of air-breathing creatures that includes spiders, ticks, mites and scorpions. Every time I see a stilt walker I think of this slow-moving, harmless arachnid. Whenever I see one backed neatly into a corner I assume that either its belly is full for the time being or that it is patiently waiting for nighttime hours when it will use the cover of darkness to prey upon live insects. They are also known to consume dead insects as well as plant juices. I have frequently encountered them, while I was picking raspberries, clinging to one of the ripe fruits, relishing some of the delectable juice.

be regenerated but the "stilt-walkers" appear to maneuver just as well on six or seven as on all eight.

Have you ever observed one of the Daddies long enough to see it "sit down?" Obviously they must do so in order to capture their food.

We have frequently watched two Daddy-long-legs performing very humorous "rumba" movements, waving their legs all the while. It finally dawned on us that one of them was really a "Mamma-long-legs!"

Place a live Daddy-long-legs in a large jar along with a couple of drops of sugar-water. How meticulously it will clean its legs, one at a time, by grasping them with one of its palpe and carefully pulling them through its jaws.

While picking Thimbleberries in past Augusts it was common to find a Harvestman practically wrapped around one of the juicy fruits with all eight legs, apparently feasting upon the nourishing liquid. They are, however, primarily insect eaters.

A female uses her ovipositor to deposit eggs as deeply as possible into the soil where they will hatch the following spring.

In several weeks, come the first hard killing frost, all that will remain of these wonderful Partners In Nature will be their eggs, viable source of those stilt-walking marvels of harvest time.

September

Insect Houdini

A few weeks ago a Walkingstick provided me with my reward for the day. Often times in past years, having returned with a group of students from a hike in the woods, we would sit down and review what we had seen and learned. Finally I would ask each student to name their favorite sighting of the outing. Naturally I came to look upon those most exciting discoveries as their rewards for the day.

Frequently the first choices turned out to be some type of animal that we came upon very unexpectedly, one that thoroughly surprised us. Usually those creatures made few sounds, often were slow moving, shy, well camouflaged, or they lived in out-of-the-way environments infrequently visited by people.

One of the very most exciting finds turned out to be a Snapping Turtle, slow, cumbersome, not about to be hurried. Invariably it had come out of one of the wet muddy swales and onto the dry sandy trail in search of a site to lay its eggs.

Porcupines and Opossums always turned up when we least expected to see them, resulting in some momentary excitement as the animals hastily made their retreat. Usually the Porcupine would climb into a nearby tree offering the group a good look — from a distance.

We consider ourselves fortunate to be living in a woods that contains many Northern Red Oaks, simply because of all the creatures that feed upon the acorns. The oaks also account for plenty of Walkingsticks because of their reputation for favoring the flesh of oak leaves. Fortunately the population of these intriguing insects is never so high in our area that it jeopardizes in any way the large hardwood trees.

No animal ever brought about such a wide range of emotions in the group as did the snake that suddenly found itself in our midst. Fortunately, living in northeastern Wisconsin, we were assured that the reptile was non-poisonous. Unfortunately this fact did little to put some of the onlookers at ease.

The Walkingstick surprised me recently in the raspberry patch. I reached down to pick a berry — and there was the 4-inch-long passive mimic, a cane without leaves. Its incredible stick-like camouflage is used only for protection from predators and not for ambushing other insects. This creature is strictly a vegetarian. As I gently tapped the raspberry cane the Walkingstick and the plant suddenly became one and the same thing.

Once confronted, the Walkingstick stretched its front legs straight ahead causing it to more closely resemble the plant on which it was resting. Young Walkingsticks are green while the adults tend to be more brownish. Their long thorax and abdomen, long threadlike antennae and long slender legs of about the same length combine to make this insect easy to identify.

Their slow deliberate movements are similar to the natural wind-caused movements of the plants making the insect and plant blend all the more. Walkingsticks become very stationary when danger approaches. In fact they are known to do most of their moving and feeding under cover of darkness. During daylight hours they tend to rest motionlessly.

This is one of few insects that can regenerate lost legs. It is easy to imagine that a creature with such long spindly appendages occasionally loses one to a predator, such as a Praying Mantis. None of the higher animals on earth are known to be capable of growing new legs.

The leaves of oak, hazelnut, locust, cherry and walnut trees number among the plant materials they consume. It is rare that damaging outbreaks of these fascinating insects occur in this part of the country. As a matter of fact, Walkingsticks tend to be quite uncommon this far north.

The specimen I enjoyed in early September appeared to be a fully-grown adult. I suspect that mating is occurring this month. About 100 eggs are dropped randomly to the ground as the female walks among the branches and foliage of trees. A quick-drying, waterproof, varnish-type fluid coats each egg when laid, thereby providing it with a highly protective case. Each oval egg is about 3 mm long and is polished-black with a whitish stripe on the side. The eggs have to be extremely durable because this is the only way Walkingsticks at this latitude survive through the winter. Hibernation is in the egg stage.

Like Grasshoppers and Field Crickets, Walkingsticks go through an incomplete metamorphosis. Nymphs hatch from the eggs and appear like miniature adults. They eat, grow, and shed their skin a few times before reaching adult size. From birth to maturity requires about six weeks.

One of the longest insects in the world is an East Indian Walkingstick whose body is around 13 inches long. With its legs outstretched it measures 20 inches! I'm aware of only one species of Walkingstick in our region, fortunately considerably shorter than the one from the East Indies!

One might call the Walkingstick the "Houdini of the Insect World," now you see it, now you don't. September would be incomplete without my being able to admire one of these fascinating insects, a recent reward in the raspberry patch.

Needle-Billed Dynamos

Several friends have recently asked me when they should take in their hummingbird feeders. Directions on one of the feeders told an owner to take the feeder down no later than September 15. Recent literature indicates that it is best to leave the filled hummingbird feeders up well into the fall season, the reason being that late-migrating hummingbirds passing through your area may receive life-saving nourishment from your sugar-water feeders.

If people were asked to list the species of birds that nest in all counties in Wisconsin I wonder how many would include the Ruby-throated Hummingbird? Yes, they do spend the summer in every county. The male shown in this photo rests on a wooden perch fastened to our deck railing within ten feet of our kitchen window. It was our good fortune that we decided to plant a long row of Salvia flowers along our front patio this spring. On several occasions I watched the female hummingbird patiently and with great speed dart from one long tubular floret to another in search of insects that were hiding within. This went on for upwards of five or more minutes, within three feet from where I stood in fascination, before she darted into the nearby woods presumably to feed the insects to her two young in the nest.

The general assumption through the years has been to take these feeders in during mid-September, the belief being that leaving them out any later might entice your hummingbirds into remaining here too long thereby decreasing their chances for a safe migration southward. Today it is felt that the hummingbirds will migrate at the proper time regardless of the food that is available to them.

The few straggler birds, including hummingbirds, that mysteriously remain at northern latitudes well into fall and even throughout the winter, always leave the "experts" guessing. A few individuals from a small flock of Brown-headed Cowbirds that was wintering one year near the twin cities in Minnesota were shot and examined and found to be suffering from encephalitis. Presumably this had prevented them from migrating normally.

I've also been asked how one goes about locating the nest of a hummingbird. Very few of these finely sculptured "works of art" are ever found compared to the thousands of hummingbirds seen and enjoyed by people of this area.   A few nests that I was invited to photograph were discovered through sheer luck, often within 20 or 30 feet of the people's home.

In several instances careful and repeated observations of the hummingbirds revealed their paths of flight from the feeders directly to their nests. As far as I can tell, these miniature marvels have no favorite trees in which to construct their nests. The two species of trees I have observed them nesting in were Northern White Cedar and Sugar Maple.

The walnut-size nest is constructed entirely by the female. Two white eggs, approximately 12.9 by 8.8 millimeters are laid. She incubates them for as many as 19 days before they hatch. The young, naked at birth, may remain in the nest for up to 25 days before leaving to develop their own food-finding skills.

How well I remember photographing a nesting Ruby-throated Hummingbird as I balanced at the top of an 8-foot stepladder at the home of Ray and Lou Hotz along the west shore of Kangaroo Lake. The sparkly, dark-eyed female scrutinized me suspiciously as I tried to be as inconspicuous as possible, not an easy feat while one is out in the open at the top of a ladder. She had built her nest on a half-inch Northern White Cedar branch liberally grown over with lichens.

Frequently she perched near the nest and either preened herself or glared at me. If she moved only an inch to one side or the other, as she often nervously did, she flew that short distance. Once she took off from the nest at what appeared to be top speed, calculated to be around 30 M.P.H., and flew directly across Kangaroo Lake. At first this surprised me but then I remembered reading that they are known to migrate nonstop across the Gulf of Mexico, at least 500 miles. Some difference!

Not once did she flinch when I clicked the shutter. Each time she came onto the nest she sat in the same direction, her head facing east, tail toward the west. My camera was focused and ready for action the instant she landed.

Later that fall I collected the nest which measured one inch high and one and one-half inches wide from edge to edge. It was slightly longer than it was wide. A common bottle cap easily covered the opening. Included among the various lichens meticulously covering and camouflaging the outer surface of the nest was the species *Parmelia sulcata*. Dr. John Thomson, lichenologist emeritus with the University of Wisconsin-Madison, examined the collection of Ruby-throated Hummingbird nests at the Milwaukee Public Museum and was surprised to learn that every one of them had *Parmelia sulcata* among the lichens on them.

Whenever we have watched hummingbirds at our feeders in the past we noticed very little movement at the wrist and elbow joints of their wings. It appears as though the birds were hovering, helicopter-style, with their wings in a plane parallel to the ground. High-speed cameras have proven that these needle-billed dynamos have a wing-beat of 50 to 70 times per second. No wonder these miniature marvels need so much energy.

Unlike what most people think, the majority of these birds' food, as much as three-fourths, consists of insects or spiders. These winged gems, the hummingbirds, find their daily fat and protein especially inside orange to reddish blossoms. They also gather some nectar, frequently transferring pollen at the same time. Deeply-tubed flowers, offering small creatures hiding places, tend to be favorites of the hummers.

The lowering air temperatures and fewer daylight hours this fall will trigger the southerly migration, as much as 2000 miles, of these deft blossom probers. They will have left us with the same thought as in previous years, that the most precious, inspiring, fascinating bird in all of eastern United States is the Ruby-throated Hummingbird.

Doll's Eyes

Hundreds of people hiking in the woods with me during early autumn in past years have looked at a fruiting plant and asked, "What kind of a berry is that?" Frequently it turned out that the fruit was not a berry but rather a pome, drupe, or drupelet.

In the technical botanical sense a berry is a fleshy or pulpy fruit that does not usually open, has few or many seeds, but no stone. It always develops from a single enlarged ovary. The berries would be a cranberry, currant, blueberry, huckleberry, baneberry, grape, tomato, and eggplant.

An example of a pome would be an apple, pear, hawthorn, and serviceberry, also called Juneberry or shadbush. A drupe is a fruit that does not split. The seed is enclosed in a bony stone, hence such fruits are often called stone fruits. Peaches, plums, cherries, and olives are drupes.

Raspberries and blackberries are really collections of tiny drupelets attached to a small receptacle. However, could you imagine calling them raspdrupelets and blackdrupelets? I can't either!

One of the most interesting photographs I have is a close-up of a thimbleberry flower showing the circle of several dozen stigmas just inside the large showy white petals. One can easily sense that each stigma, when pollinated, will lead to the development of one seed.

When you pick a tangy thimbleberry or raspberry the mass of drupelets parts from the receptacle, and the fruit is hollow. The mass of drupelets on a blackberry adheres to the small fleshy receptacle which is part of the berry and is eaten with it.

One of the most striking and eye-catching of the true berries found growing in the cool shady woods, the White Baneberry, adorns the late summer landscape from mid-August into September. These hardy native perennials with the showy spikes of white berries are said to be mildly poisonous, hence the name of baneberry.

Personally speaking I find it difficult to imagine something being mildly poisonous. In my estimation it is either poisonous or non-poisonous. I have told many hundreds of school children, during our September hikes in the woods, that the White Baneberries are very poisonous. In fact I found it a good time to introduce them to the word "bane" meaning "that which destroys life."

Many people call this attractive plant Doll's Eyes. The fruit is a four or five-inch-long cluster of loosely-spaced oval white berries, each with a dark purple to black spot on the end, the bold spot formed where the broad stigma was attached.

The story is that the berries resembled the old-fashioned china eyes that small children so frequently managed to gouge from their dolls' heads, hence the name "Doll's Eyes."

The ivory-toned berries are supported on much-thickened reddish pedicels and peduncles. The pedicel (PED-i-sell) is the short stalk to which the berry is fastened, while the peduncle (PEA-dunk-ul) is the central stalk from which emanate the individual pedicels. Because the plant may

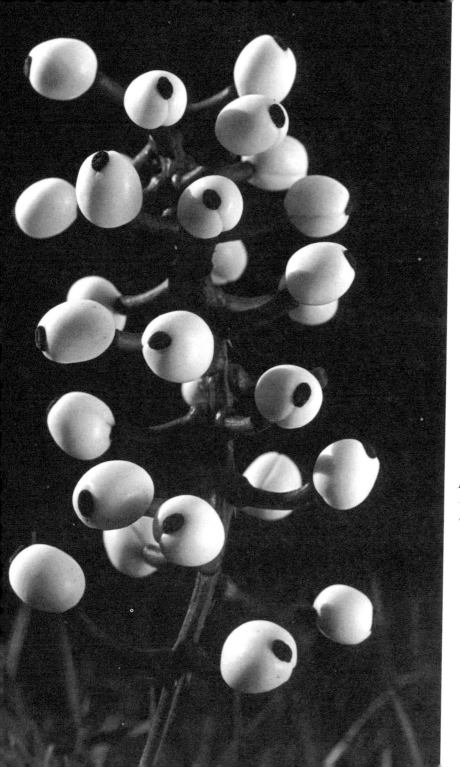

The various wild fruits of autumn add greatly to the elegant tapestry of the woods and its borders. It's often the pure white fruits, such as the White Baneberry or Doll's Eyes, that stand out so boldly and capture one's attention. Occasionally one comes upon White Baneberries that, rather than being supported on the typical brilliant pink stalks, are attached to thin wiry stalks. These are hybrids between the White Baneberry, having fleshy pink stalks, and the Red Baneberry that has thin wiry stalks.

grow as tall as three feet, it strikes a very imposing picture against the more earthy greens and browns of the fall woods.

Linnaeus named the plant *Actaea* (ak-TEE-a), the ancient name of the Elder. Its species name, *pachypoda* (pa-KIP-o-da), means thick-footed in allusion to the thick, brilliant red pedicels.

Muenschner, in his excellent book, *Poisonous Plants of the United States,* tells about someone's experience of consuming six of the white baneberries which, in turn, produced increased pulse, dizziness, burning in the stomach, and colicky pains. The rootstalk is a violent purgative, irritant and emetic.

Occasionally one comes across the Red Baneberry, *Actaea rubra* (RUE-bra), which has a more globular cluster of very shiny red berries supported on thin pedicels. Frequently the white variety (referred to as *A. neglecta*) is more abundant than the red. These white berries have smaller black "dots" and also the thin pedicels of the red species. It is thought that this is a hybrid between the White and the Red Baneberries.

One of the few animals reputed to eat the berries of the Doll's Eyes is the Ruffed Grouse. I trust that the grouse, during its wanderings, will inadvertently scatter the seeds of the Doll's Eyes which will germinate, grow and emblazon the forest with their handsome red and white ornaments.

A Caterpillar, Dressed

A story about a butterfly unfolds at this time of the year adding a new dimension to one's understanding of these fragile insects. One scholarly American lepidopterist (one who studies butterflies and moths) of years ago described them as "frail children of the air." There are several species, however, that would surely rear up their wings, could they communicate verbally with us, and voice disagreement with this depiction.

Anglewings, Red Admirals, Painted Ladies, Milbert's and Compton's Tortoise-shells, and Mourning Cloaks are almost supernatural butterflies in their ability to overwinter as adults in this area. They may be frail of body but not when it comes to withstanding temperatures of 30 degrees below zero F.!

The story of the Mourning Cloak butterfly begins in mid-March. An unusually warm day greets us as we make our way into the maple woods, snow still covering quite a bit of the ground, to observe one of the grandest rituals of all, the making of pure maple syrup. One of our most unexpected surprises of the day turns out to be an adult Mourning Cloak butterfly sipping Sugar Maple sap from a twig broken by a winter storm.

The adults, having emerged from their cocoons the previous August or early September, crawled under a piece of loose bark on a tree or, better yet, between logs of a pile of firewood being dried for next year's use, to spend the winter. The wings and body of these three-inch-wide butterflies are deep purplish-brown, velvety, and in fact quite hairy. Even the surfaces of their eyes are covered by fine hairs. A broad yellow band on the outer margins of their wings is highlighted by a row of light blue spots, as seen from above, just inside the band. Undoubtedly their body and wing hairs serve as insulation during their long winter dormancy.

Mourning Cloaks tend to be double-brooded in the South and single-brooded in their northern range. They inhabit a wide area of Europe, Asia and North America. The discovery of their chrysalises here only in late summer leads me to believe they are single-brooded in our area. There is evidence that the adult Mourning Cloaks become lethargic during the heat of summer and are quite inactive. The new adults will survive the winter, mate next summer and then die. They will have existed as adults for about 10 months.

A butterfly that so trustingly and tamely alights on your hand surely must be included on one's list of favorite wild creatures. Although other species of butterflies, including the Baltimore Checkerspot and the Painted Lady, have taken a liking to the salts and whatever else was contained in my perspiration, the Mourning Cloak has confided in my presence and landed on me most frequently.

Having mated, the female will lay eggs in clusters of about 20 encircling a twig of one of the caterpillars' host foods. This is usually American Elm, willow or one of the poplars such as Quaking Aspen, Balsam Poplar or Eastern Cottonwood.

The eggs hatch about two weeks later into little black hairy caterpillars. Now begins the larval stage. Upon hatching they crawl to the nearest leaf and line up, side by side, with their heads facing outward and begin eating the leaf.

About a week later they will molt for the first time. The skin will split down the back and out will crawl the slightly larger caterpillar with the new coat that had formed below the old, bristly hairs and all. This molting process will be repeated three times during the next three weeks, the larvae increasing in size with each molt. The growth-period between one molt and the next is called an instar.

Apparently one of the Quaking Aspen trees near the edge of our property was used by a female Mourning Cloak as her "nursery" during early August. A month later, the fourth molt completed, the fully-grown caterpillars headed in various directions in search of suitable sites for that critical event, the chrysalis state, during which they would undergo that miraculous metamorphosis, changing from caterpillar to adult butterfly.

Much to our joy 15 of the caterpillars chose the east and south sides of our house, from three to 11 feet above the ground, as their pupal retreats. Each larva spun a tiny pad-like web of silk usually on the underside of one of the clapboards or windowsills. This silk came from a small tubular opening called a spinneret, located on the lower lip.

Next the caterpillar arched its body upward entangling the hooked claws of its hind legs in the silk, then letting its body hang down with the head end curved slightly upward. Several hours later the skin along its back began to split just behind its head. Gradually the thin spiny skin worked upward as the caterpillar wriggled. Finally the little shriveled mass of skin either fell to the ground or stuck to some of the webbing and remained there.

Now this peculiar looking grayish-brown object, the chrysalis, hung as quietly and inert as a mummy. Several of those I touched wriggled vigorously, then resumed their quite helpless position.

The adults emerged, one by one, from their paper-thin mummy shells about two weeks later. Each clung to its empty case while its wings hung limply downward. Slowly it reached its full length and the butterfly began exercising, opening and closing the newly formed wings, until finally it flew away. John Gay summed it up perfectly in 1727 when he wrote, "And what's a butterfly? At best, he's but a caterpillar, dressed."

Warm days in fall will find the adults out of their hiding places in search of food such as nectar from asters or even the sugary sweetness from rotting apple "windfalls" lying on the ground. The arrival of cold weather will force them into their hideaways for five or six months.

Tree sap, willow catkins, Trailing Arbutus and Moosewood shrub flowers will provide the adults with their first food in spring. A succession of blossoming periods, including cherry and apple trees, will supply them with plenty of nourishment for the next several months until mating occurs and they will have reached the end of their lives.

Henry David Thoreau wrote, "Nature is mythical and mystical always, and spends her whole genius on the least work." An average human being, weighing about 120,000 times more than the exquisite dark-winged beauty, can gaze at a chrysalis during the first hints of autumn knowing that here marks the beginning of an intriguing 10-month-long drama, the life cycle of a Mourning Cloak butterfly.

Woodland Drummer

Charlotte, the mushroom expert in our family, frequently learns of some special or unusual specimens growing in the county. A recent phone call alerted her to three Giant Puffballs growing on someone's front lawn, so away we went equipped with cameras and whatever else was required to study the large fungi.

And they were huge, the largest being 10 inches high and 14 inches across. Not having permission, we did not collect any of the puffballs for eating. Hopefully they will remain intact so we can photograph them in various stages of growth and deterioration.

David Arora, author of *Mushrooms Demystified*, our most favorite of all mushroom books, wrote, "*Calvatias* are among the most prolific of living organisms. It has been calculated that an average-sized (30cm or 12 inches) specimen of the Giant Puffball (*Calvatia gigantea*) contains 7,000,000,000,000 (7 trillion) spores! In these inflationary times that may not sound like much, but consider this: if all 7 trillion spores (each one measuring 1/200 of a millimeter) were lined up in a row, they would circle the earth's equator! If each spore produced a 30 cm offspring, the resulting puffballs would stretch from the earth to the sun and back, and if their spores were equally successful, the formidable puffball mass would weigh 800 times as much as the earth! Each spore is theoretically capable of germinating, yet very few (obviously!) do. It would be interesting to know why so many don't, or conversely, why such a surplus of spores is (needlessly?) produced."

Arora goes on to say, "Because of its preference for open hillsides, it (Giant Puffball) can often be spotted from the road. Large specimens, in fact, have been mistaken by passersby for

An incredible triangle of Giant Puffballs finds Charlotte Lukes kneeling in joy and amaze-ment. Perhaps it is because these huge, safe-to-eat, globular fungi (FUN-ji) are so easy to identify that many people enjoy consuming them. When asked how they prepare them, one of our friends replied, "I dip thin slices of the puffball in a milk-egg mixture, dredge them in soda cracker crumbs and finally fry them lightly in a little butter." Charlotte then asked her how they tasted, and her reply was, "like fried soda cracker crumbs!"

herds of grazing sheep! (Mushroom hunters, on the other hand, are more likely to mistake grazing sheep for Giant Puffballs.)"*

Our enjoyable incident with the three Giant Puffballs brought back memories of one of my most cherished and unusual experiences I have ever had with a fungus. My favorite boyhood hiking area near my hometown of Kewaunee, Wisconsin took me through the hilly woods to the south of the Kewaunee River, a place I dearly missed during the years I was away at college and in the army.

I headed for "my" woods on a crisp sunny Saturday afternoon one September. A high hill with a clear scenic view toward the river became my lunch stop and helped to bring back dozens of pleasant memories, especially of the many adventures my friend, Tony Kotyza, and I had there as boys.

All of a sudden a very strange far-away sound reached my ears, "Thump....thump....thump....thump." The only object I could associate with the sound was a large hollow rubber ball being bounced upon a sidewalk, hardly possible here in the middle of a woods over a mile from the nearest road.

The mysterious beat continued and became louder and louder, somewhat like the cadence of a small bass drum. Suddenly two figures appeared over the rise of the next hill, a man and a little boy. Now I could see that the youngster was carrying something whitish under one of his arms and was giving it a good solid whack about once every four steps.

Finally they approached me, stopped for a chat, and showed me with great pride the giant puffball they had found along the way. This was the mysterious "drum" I had been hearing and the little boy was the drummer!

Of all the fungi in the world, few are as easy to identify and as safe to eat as the large puff-ball, *Calvatia* (cal-VAY-she-a) *gigantea* (jy-GAN-tee-a). However, I can easily visualize a careless person picking a nice solid mushroom in the small button stage, before the cap develops, assuming that it is a very young puffball, and eating by mistake one of the deadly *Amanita* mushrooms.

There are several things you can do to avoid a drastic mistake, in fact perhaps your last mistake! Use only the large puffballs for food, those which are grapefruit size or larger. Cut through the globe-shaped fungus from top to bottom. The color of the flesh must be perfectly white in order to be edible. In fact eating a puffball that has begun to turn color and to deteriorate may make you very ill.

Secondly, this cross section will enable you to check for tiny pinholes which will indicate the presence of small worms. They too are very fond of these choice morsels. The least bit of darkening indicates that the puffball is beginning to develop mature spores. This dried spore mass was used for many years by barber-surgeons as a styptic to stop bleeding. Some people in the olden days used bits of dried puffballs as tinder, while the Finns used this fungus as a cure for diarrhea in calves.

Theoretically one spore, planted by natural forces in the proper rich wet humus, can result in a tremendously large puffball. A vast series of extremely thin cobweb-like mycelia (my-SEE-lee-a), growing into the ground and consuming organic material, will develop from the single spore. This is in reality the vegetative portion of all fungi including those that are gilled, woody or otherwise. Eventually, much like a blossom on a rose bush, the proper combination of moisture, heat and other growing conditions will result in the so-called fruiting body, the mushroom or puffball itself.

One old English name for the puffball was fuss ball and may have been the forerunner of the word "football." Schoolboys were known to enjoy kicking large mature fuss balls to cause them to "smoke," and to scatter the dust-like spores. By the way, inhaling a great quantity of these spores can cause a severe lung infection.

Puffballs have for centuries been known to stimulate gourmets' salivary glands and excite wonder in the lucky finder. Our favorite way of eating them is to cut them into half-inch-thick slices, thoroughly coat them with a mixture of beaten egg and milk, dip in soda cracker crumbs and lightly sauté in butter.

Henry David Thoreau wrote, "If a man does not keep pace with his companions, perhaps it is because he hears a different drummer. Let him step to the music which he hears, however measured or far away." This brings me back to that gorgeous September day and the mysterious and enchanting music a little boy, in tune with nature, drummed for me on a puffball.

October

Nature's Spirals

It was while sitting on the couch at the home of our friends, Dick and Ginny Haen, that a story idea popped into my head. On the wall opposite from where Charlotte and I sat were arranged beautiful pictures, several heirloom items and a lovely old cuckoo clock. The classic clock was the kind that was interestingly powered by small chains and weights that hung downward. As is customary, the weights were patterned after Norway Spruce cones.

I immediately thought back to my early childhood when my Dad would often take my three brothers and me out to visit his Uncle Joseph Lukes north of Kewaunee. We boys loved to visit our great uncle for two reasons. His several cuckoo clocks fascinated us as did his wonderful, lively, old-fashioned button-accordion playing. The cuckoo clocks at his log farm-home also were powered by "spruce cone" weights.

The patterning of the cuckoo clock weights after the cones of the Norway Spruce supposedly dates back several centuries to the cuckoo clock makers of the Black Forest in Europe. The dark somber spruces that predominated at that time there, giving the forest its "Black" name, were the Norway Spruces, *Picea Abies* (PIE-see-a A-bee-eez).

The study of spirals in nature can be intriguing, including those of the Norway Spruce cones pictured here. Another excellent, easy-to-study example of "Fibonacci's Spirals" is the sunflower, especially one of the large-flowered varieties.

Norway Spruces grow wild throughout Europe and prefer fertile soil, moist air and cool shady valleys. Their fast-growing nature, narrow conical crowns and spectacular spire-like shape have made them extremely popular in northern United States for a couple of centuries or more. The largest specimens in our country frequently are seen in parks, cemeteries, on private grounds or in windbreaks surrounding farm buildings on the prairies.

The wood of this tree is finely grained and is of a homogeneous texture. It transmits sound so well that for centuries it has been used in the manufacture of violins, other stringed instruments and the sounding boards of pianos. Norway Spruces are still considered to be the traditional Christmas tree throughout much of Europe today.

Several characteristics make these trees easy to identify. Their branches droop down, then curve gracefully up toward the tips. Cones of the Norway Spruce can be four to seven inches long, considerably larger than those of the three species of spruces native to northeastern United States, the red, black and white. As an interpretive naturalist I always referred to the beautiful cones of the Norway Spruce as the "cuckoo clock cones."

Examine a cone of this spruce tree and you will easily see that its wedge-shaped, ragged scales are arranged so as to form two different spirals going in opposite directions for the entire length of the cone. It was an Italian mathematician, Leonardo Fibonacci, who elaborated on this design. Fibonacci (fib-o-NAH-chee), who lived from 1170 to 1230, apparently was fascinated by the spirals of nature. These could be seen in the petals of a flower, the seed arrangement on a sunflower head, scales of an evergreen cone, thorns on a rose bush, as well as the leaves of many garden vegetables.

The mathematical progression produced what is now referred to as the Fibonacci series: 1, 1, 2, 3, 5, 8, 13, 21, 34, 55, 89, 144, 233, 377 and so on. Notice that each number is the sum of the two preceding numbers.

If a fraction is made using successive numbers, for example 13/21 or 21/34, the denominator always turns out to be 1.618 times that of the numerator. The Golden Ratio, 1.618, referred to as *phi*, is in honor of Phidias, the famous ancient Greek sculptor. The long side of the Parthenon in Greece is 1.618 times the shorter side!

The leathery scales of the Norway Spruce, like the sunflower seeds in a single head, are arranged in two distinct spirals, one clockwise and the other counterclockwise. Using a piece of string, follow the edges of the shallow spiral first. You should be able to encircle the cone about four or five times. Invariably there will be five rows of scales within each complete spiral.

Following the more steeply-pitched spiral you should discover there to be eight rows of scales between each complete spiral. These two sets of spirals are said to have a 5/8 arrangement. Look back at the Fibonacci series to see that five and eight are indeed consecutive numbers in that symmetrical and uniform ratio!

The basic plan of trees, the spacing of their twigs, leaves and needles, is another fine example of the beauty and function of nature's spirals, in this case enabling the trees to take maximum advantage of the sun's energy. Twigs and leaves of maples and ashes have opposite arrangement. Those on the Linden (Basswood) tree are not opposite but rather spiral in such a way that a 180 degree angle separates each twig.

From the amazing Chambered Nautilus shell to the lowly Oxeye Daisy, well-proportioned design based upon spirals has proven to be the most efficient arrangement in nature. The Evening Grosbeaks and Black-capped Chickadees eating sunflower seeds at our feeders today couldn't care less about the Fibonacci series.

Humans, however, with their ability to learn and think, should take great delight in the intricate designs nature has provided, spirals included.

Ancient Tree Of Life

The thought of locating a living Northern White Cedar that began growing here in a crevice along the precipitous dolostone bluff more than 500 years before the arrival of Christopher Columbus excites us immensely.

Late Woodland Indians of this region around 960 A.D. apparently knew the fine qualities of this cedar as is shown in their lightweight durable canoes. The ribs, prows, frames and gunwales of these craft were made of this wood.

The annual rings, or yearly growth thicknesses, sometimes pull apart in living trees due to wind-shake. The Native Americans, knowing this, used a stout club to pound the cut lengths of cedar in order to loosen these annual thicknesses into thin flexible strips.

The Indians call this pungent aromatic tree "Os-soo-ha-tah," meaning feather leaf. French voyageurs in North America learned from the Indians during the late 1500's that a potent tea brewed from the leaves and bark of this tree, rich in vitamin C, cured scurvy like magic. This quality perhaps led to its being the first North American tree to be introduced to Europe. There is record of one planted in Paris in 1553.

Our Native American friend, Keewaydenoquay, and her people on Garden Island in northern Lake Michigan have for many generations honored the Northern White Cedar as their sacred tree. Beauty, durability, fragrance, historical importance, medicinal properties, long life, usefulness to people and wildlife – this tree has them all.

Professor Douglas Larson, teacher and researcher at the University of Guelph in Ontario, Canada, had been studying the ages of Northern White Cedars, especially those growing on the

This old cliff-hugging Northern White Cedar towers over its dedicated custodian, Bob Yeomans, standing on the rocky northern Door County shore about 20 feet below where the venerable giant grows. Even without having attempted to scientifically age this tree, my guess is that it is in the neighborhood of 300 or more years old.

Bruce Peninsula and nearby islands. The researchers' goal is to use this data to attempt to create a living analogue for the past 1,000 years of Ontario's environmental conditions.

Their studies have found that some of the oldest living Northern White Cedars are no more than 21 feet tall. In some years of poor growth the new wood laid down was only two cells thick. We think of only mosses and lichens of this region growing as slowly.

Prior to the start of this study, Larson was of the opinion that the maximum age of a Northern White Cedar, *Thuja* (THEW-ya) *occidentalis* (ok-si-den-TAY-lis), was between 300 and 400 years. Suddenly an in-depth examination of the trees began turning up specimens more than 700 years old, then 800 and 900!

Finally, on Bear's Rump Island off the east coast of the Bruce Peninsula jutting out into Lake Huron, they discovered a rather small, gnarled, twisted Northern White Cedar, clinging tenaciously to the cliff face, that was 1,032 years old! And here is where 960 A.D. enters this story, the approximate year when this durable tree began its life.

Dendrochronologists, (den-dro-cro-NOL-o-jists) those who study annual rings in tree trunks or ancient building timbers, have found the Sitka Spruce and Western Red Cedar to grow to about 2,000 years of age. Bald Cypresses of the South commonly reach 1,000 years, but the "Methuselah" of them all is the Bristlecone Pine of the high, dry, cold western mountains that has been known to grow to 5,000 years of age.

Larson's group has had the best luck in aging these old trees by studying complete cross sections of the cedars that, due to rock slides or other natural causes, had been carried, uprooted, to the bottom of the cliffs. A coring tool, called an increment borer, can harmlessly remove a drinking-straw-size core from a living tree to be used in the aging process. This is a difficult process at best, especially when absolute accuracy is important.

One hears a lot about the old-growth forests of the West, especially regarding the fate of the rare Spotted Owl, but rarely thinks of old-growth trees existing in northeastern Wisconsin. Many of the old Northern White Cedars have disappeared because of logging, forest fires and clearing for settlement and development.

Unfortunately most cedar swamps are merely tolerated instead of being managed. The majority are clear-cut, drained and filled in, and a usually unsuccessful attempt is made to grow crops on the land. Many of these swamps could be put to their best use as good natural underground reservoirs and efficient natural water purifiers.

The soil there has outstanding water-holding capacity and would help greatly to temper stream flow and regulate and produce more uniform precipitation. Selective cutting could be done from year to year, providing the owner with reasonable compensation.

We long to see the national record Northern White Cedar some day, directly across Lake Michigan to the east in Leelanau County, Michigan. It measures 18 feet in circumference (4 1/2 feet above the ground), is 113 feet high and has an average crown spread of 42 feet.

We will search this part of the state diligently within the next few years for a living Northern White Cedar that surpasses 1,000 years in age. Undoubtedly this old veteran of thousands of storms and full moons will be found growing out of harm's way but also being exposed to extremely poor growing conditions. Fortunately it will have been inaccessible to the cutters and developers for many years.

Hopefully, having found such a prize, we will recommend all the more that the owners of these valuable trees work hard at being good caretakers of their land and trees as have our friends, Bob and Charlotte Yeomans, who are such excellent stewards of their beautiful old-growth Northern White Cedar bluff land.

It's high time that we as humans choose a sacred tree and a sacred sky and a sacred earth!

Among the pine family in North America, only the Tamarack, Larch and Bald Cypress are deciduous. All others retain most of their needles (modified leaves) throughout the winter. Even though many tree books refer to this tree as the American Larch, I prefer the name of Tamarack. The Native Americans of this region called it the Hackmatack, and that wonderful name would satisfy me completely.

The Golden Conifers

Typical of the oaks, there is a Northern Red Oak near our front yard that is clinging to its leaves tenaciously. I look at one leaf being twirled round and round by the wind and wonder how long it can be subjected to such constant stress before it finally comes loose and falls to the ground.

Suddenly one does come off and sails downward in much the same fashion as a well-made paper airplane. Few trees, in my estimation, produce dried leaves having better "loft time" when they fall than the Northern Red oak.

Some day, just for the fun of it, I am going to organize a leaf sailing contest, or picnic, in early November. We'll each take our entries to the top of the tall observation tower at the Peninsula State Park and, like runners starting a race, on signal, drop our leaves. The object will be to see whose leaves require the longest time to reach the ground. In other words, the last one to reach the ground, or the "finish line," will be the winner. (Why must the fastest always be the winner?)

There is another tree that has been colored to perfection and is just now beginning to gracefully drop its leaves, the American Tamarack. Their magnificent "smoky gold" performance being staged now would be quite insignificant if many of the deciduous trees, such as the maples, birches and ashes, would also be at their peak of color. Fortunately the Tamaracks have the entire stage to themselves, front and center.

Many call them larches even though they are distinctly different in several ways than the European Larch and the Western (US) Larch. The Native Americans, particularly those of the great Algonquin Nation, referred to them as "Hackmatacks." No one seems to know the derivation of the word Tamarack. In fact *Webster's Third International Dictionary* simply says, "origin unknown" while the *American Heritage Dictionary* says it is from Algonquin. I prefer to call them Tamaracks because the word sounds a little like Hackmatack.

Wisconsin's Tamarack swamps and bogs of years ago must have been very impressive. A terrible invasion and infestation, perhaps from the North, of the Larch Sawfly, *Pristophora ericksonii*, between 1900 and 1910 killed millions of Wisconsin's and neighboring state's Tamaracks. We are admiring the considerably smaller second generation trees today.

What were the dimensions of those big mature "Hackmatacks" at the turn of the century? Well, today's record in Wisconsin is about 9.5 feet in circumference and 85 feet tall. The national record, growing today in Maine, is 12.25 feet around and stands 92 feet tall.

I think back fondly to my high school days in Kewaunee and one of the football and basketball stars whom everyone called "Tamarack," usually "Tam" for short. The qualities of Tamarack wood are: heavy, hard, very strong, coarse-grained and unusually durable. Every one of these characteristics fit "Tamarack" Hlinak (LIN-yok in Czech.)to a "T!"

It was Miss Emma Toft who advised me, when I began heating my house with a wood stove in 1966, to never burn Tamarack in the old cast iron "Queen." "Burns much too hot," she said, "and will in time ruin the stove grates."

Look for Black Spruces, *Picea mariana*, wherever Tamaracks grow. They are true partners of the swamps and bogs. Both do quite well in cold wet habitats, and neither can stand shade from other trees. In fact the Tamarack doesn't even like to be crowded by its own kind.

The American Tamarack, *Larix laricina* (LAIR-ix lair-i-SY-na), is considered to be the most northern-growing conifer on this continent, growing north in Mackenzie to the Arctic Circle, around 67 Degrees N. Latitude, and thriving there by the light of the midnight sun.

Its counterpart in Asia, *Larix sibirica* (si-BIR-i-ca), produces the most northern coniferous forest in the entire world in Siberia at 72 degrees N. Latitude. Talk about being hardy. This is approximately the same latitude as the very northern tip of Alaska.

Notice that I said coniferous (cone-bearing) as opposed to evergreen. The last living evergreen tree northward on this continent is the Black Spruce, not quite as far north as the Tamarack.

A close inspection of Tamarack needles on a tree shows that they grow in clusters from tiny knobs or butts called "short shoots." By mid-November the needles will have fallen, leaving the trees naked — genuine deciduous conifers. The other two in the world are the Bald Cypress and Dawn Redwood.

The Tamarack is said to reach its pinnacle of perfection north of Lake Winnipeg in Canada. That site is on my "Must See" list for future years along with the high valleys and lower mountain slopes, between 2000 and 7000 feet, of northern Montana and Idaho where the tallest larches in the world grow, the Western Larch, *Larix occidentalis* (ok-si-den-TAY-lis), of the Western World.

I can't admire a stand of golden Tamaracks on a sunny November day without getting the feeling that they are phosphorescent, that they actually glow from their own power source. The brilliant swamp I enjoy most each fall is seen from what I call a "shunpike," a circuitous, off-the-beaten-track road at least 125 feet above the glorious Tamaracks. It's one of those lonely roads not to be advertised for fear that it would soon lose its charm and beauty because of bumper-to-bumper crowds.

Autumn's finale is reaching its zenith, and, lucky for all of us, it is occurring in the wetlands, the areas least likely to be developed, where mosquitoes reign supreme throughout the warm months.

Head for the swamps and fill your eyes with gold!

Acorns And Oaks

I like to think there was rejoicing among the wild animals recently following the extraordinarily strong winds. My guess is that many tons of acorns were shaken to the ground, there to be eaten by at least two dozen or more species of wild creatures among the nearly 100 that are known to consume acorns on this continent.

Wood Ducks, Ruffed Grouse, Wild Turkeys, Blue Jays, Black Bears and Raccoons rank near the top of wildlife using the delectable nuts of oaks as food. It's not that acorns are the top priority food of these and other animals in the wild, but that this staple is so widespread and abundantly available in most years.

It wouldn't take you very long to learn, just as did wild animals, the Native Americans and early settlers, that acorns from White Oaks are far superior for eating than those obtained from Northern Red Oaks. Do you suppose that the meat of squirrels that ate White Oak acorns would be better tasting than from those squirrels that consumed Northern Red Oak acorns?

Red Oak acorns are quite bitter to the taste due to the rather high amount of tannin they contain. However, the tannin, being water soluble, can be quite readily leached out of these acorns. Euell Gibbons, in his book, *Stalking the Wild Asparagus,* refers to the acorn as "an ancient food of Man" and tells how to effectively remove tannin from Red Oak acorns and use them as food.

White oaks are not bitter and can be eaten raw when they are ripe. No doubt you will prefer them roasted. A long time ago, when it was more customary to allow pigs to find their own food in the woods during certain seasons, it was said that "acorns are a delight to little children as well as pigs."

The Gray Squirrels in our woods have begun nipping off oak twigs containing small acorns by mid-August. Our graveled driveway is virtually littered by the end of October with not only the large acorns but with hundreds of foot-long twigs as well, all chewed off by the squirrels. The professional arborists warn people to not prune their oaks until a few hard frosts have occurred in the area, for fear that the sap will attract the beetles which in turn help spread the dreaded Oak Wilt Disease. Can one assume that the gray squirrels may be responsible for also spreading the disease that may kill the very trees upon which they depend for much of their food?

We happen to live in that part of Wisconsin where only Northern Red Oaks can be found growing naturally. Farther south and to the west in the state both the Red and the White Oaks occur.

Here are some ways you can easily tell them apart. Red Oaks belong to what is described as the Black Oak group including species such as the Northern Red, Scarlet, Pin, Black and Scrub Oaks. These trees have sharp-pointed winter buds and the leaves have more or less pointed lobes with bristle tips. The leaves are nearly as smooth below as above. This tree's bark is usually quite dark. The acorns ripen in two years and consequently you will see some small acorns on the trees during the winter.

White Oaks belong to the White Oak group containing species such as White, Bur and Chestnut Oak. Their leaves, which have rounded lobes without bristle tips, are rather dull and non-reflective especially on the undersides. Winter buds are blunt and the bark is usually quite light-colored, hence the name White Oak. Its acorns ripen in one year. Therefore there will be no acorns on these trees in winter.

A Northern Red Oak acorn tends to bulge near the tip and has a flat saucer-like cup at its base. They can be up to about one inch long. White Oak acorns are a little shorter, oblong, and are borne directly on the twig in a bowl-like cup covered with warty scales. Bur Oak acorns can be larger than White Oak acorns and have a fringed cap covering the lower half of the nut.

It is said that an oak may not begin producing acorns until it is 40 to 50 years old and will not reach maturity until it is about 100 years of age. Given good growing conditions it can live to be 300 or more years.

There is a magnificent Bur Oak growing not too far from where I lived, at 333 Wisconsin Ave., in Oshkosh while I attended the University there in the early 1950's. More than once I walked several blocks out of my way just to admire that majestic specimen. What a physical and spiritual uplifting I received while in the presence of that wonderful giant of a tree. As is so often said, it was a symbol of strength and loyalty. Its grandeur meant so much to me after being cooped up in school all day. I believe if I owned that prize I would make special provisions to ensure its protection in future years.

David Everett wrote in 1791 the memorable lines, "Large streams from little fountains flow, Tall oaks from little acorns grow." I think of the possibility of one of the acorns now on the ground germinating next spring and hopefully, during the next 100 years, growing into an imposing landmark of an oak, producing thousands of acorns, feeding many wild creatures and planting other oaks at Houby Hill, our present home.

Ruby Of The Muskeg

Here is a fall trivia question to tax your imagination: "What was the first Native American fruit thought to have been eaten in Europe, grows on small woody shrubs, will produce around one and one-half million barrels this fall in the United States and can be made into what is considered one of three genuine 'All-American' pies?" (Answer: the Cranberry!)

Even though most people regard either the tart cherry or apple as the genuine All-American pie, neither is native to this continent. The three native fruits of our continent that could conceivably end up in mouth-watering pies are the Blueberry, Cranberry and Concord Grape. In the case that most, if not all, of you have never heard of a Cranberry pie, I suggest that you look on page 75 of Euell Gibbons' famous book, *Stalking the Wild Asparagus*, for his tantalizing recipe for cranberry chiffon pie. I can't wait until Charlotte tries out what sounds like a winning pie recipe.

There are few native plants which I have had more fun with through the years in my nature interpretation than the woody shrub the Native Americans called "sour berry" and the Pilgrims nicknamed "ruby of the bog." I point out the exquisitely small four-petaled pink flowers in June while informing the visitors, "Everyone in this group has eaten the fruit of these small evergreen shrubs." Finally after giving my last hint, "November," they all answer, "Cranberries!"

The wild cranberry I am most familiar with is the, Small-fruited or Northern Cranberry, *Vaccinium Oxycoccos* (vack-SY-nee-um ok-si-COCK-us). I also like another name, "fruit of the muskeg." This reflects the North Country, home of this tart fruit.

Wild Cranberries hide in quaking bogs and peat swamps, out-of-the-way habitats seldom visited by the average person, and consequently it is highly unlikely that anyone would ever serve you wild cranberry sauce. The Pilgrims were presented with a goodwill offering of Cranberries by the Indians, and the white people have enjoyed them ever since.

By September and well into late fall you can be nibbling wild Cranberries. As a matter of fact most people don't care for more than a very small taste. They are extremely sour and nearly inedible when raw, but are very pleasant when cooked. By the way, one teaspoonful of salt takes the place of half the sugar (a cupful) ordinarily used with a quart of Cranberries.

Tart is indeed a good description of their taste, but add a little sweetening (Native Americans used maple sugar) and they become piquant, pleasantly tart having a lively charm.

Fruits of the Small Cranberry are about currant-size, from one-quarter to one-third inch in diameter and are often spotted with brown. The quarter-inch-long leaves are pointed, dark green above and whitish below, and are evergreen. These creeping prostrate shrubs surely have to be among the smallest, if not the smallest, woody evergreen shrubs in the United States.

A railroad crew some years ago soon came to love old Johnie Frog, an Ojibwe Indian who lived in the Flambeau area. They never tired of hearing Johnie pronounce Cranberry pie in his native language. Unfortunately for Johnie, the Ojibwes had no single word meaning pie so he had to interpret the concoction as "swamp berries made into sauce rolled between bread." Imagine

The average American unhesitatingly would say that the All-American pie is either the apple or the cherry pie, neither of which is native to America! Pictured here is the cranberry, one of three native fruits that might qualify for being made into the All-American pie. The others are the concord grape and blueberry.

having to pronounce, "mucki giminun backe minacigun wiwegido sigun" every time you wanted to say Cranberry pie! Little wonder those old railroad cronies had a good laugh whenever they could trick Johnie into saying it.

Native Americans not only ate the berry, they learned that the steeped leaves produced a tea for a person ill with nausea, and the bitter and astringent leaves could also be used in treating diarrhea and diabetes as well as for purifying the blood. Hundreds of years of trial and error led those people into using various plants for medicines which, when tested by modern day pharmacists, proved to be about 65% accurate!

It is generally the Large or American Cranberry, *Vaccinium macrocarpon,* meaning large-fruited, which is commercially grown in the United States. Several varieties, such as McFarlin, Searls, Beckwirh, Stevens and Wilcox are planted. Fruits of the American are roughly twice or more the size of the Small Cranberry and range in color from pink to dark red, mottled with red and white.

Another close relative of the Small and the American Cranberries is the Cowberry or Mountain Cranberry, also called the Lingonberry, *Vaccinium Vitis-Idaea* (vack-SY-nee-um vy-tis eye-da-EE-a). Originally this fruit was called the Grape of Mt. Ida. It can be found in extreme northern Minnesota, the mountains of the Northeast and especially on the Gaspé Peninsula and north shore of the Gulf of St. Lawrence.

Most of our Ligonberries are imported today from Newfoundland where they are called Partridgeberries, and from Norway where they are called "Lingon Baer." These fruits overwinter quite well and may be best in early spring. At least they shouldn't be picked until the frost has mellowed them.

The next most wonderful thing to eating Cranberries is seeing them in flower. The relatively long stamens and stigma of each flower resemble a crane's bill. Originally the fruit was called Craneberry and later shortened to Cranberry. Come next early July, visit a commercial Cranberry bog, west of Wisconsin Rapids in Wood County for example, to experience a "sea of pink" you'll never forget.

Come Thanksgiving Day, this delectable fruit will never have tasted so good. And I wager that thereafter you will not want to miss a single year of their flowering season. Piquant!

November

Praying For Prey

An alert person at the Sister Bay Yacht Club and Resort helped me to re-live one of the most interesting experiences I have ever had during the past 40+ years of helping people of all ages learn more about nature.

The phone call told of a Praying Mantis being seen on the outside wall of the yacht club. Yes, they had captured it! My first question was, "Are you sure it isn't a Walkingstick?" After being assured that indeed it was a Praying Mantis, and me biting my tongue for asking the doubting question, I got to wondering what on earth a genuine Praying Mantis was doing as far north in the state as Sister Bay.

Within a few days the beautiful three-inch-long European Mantid, *Mantis religiosa* (re-lij-e-O-sa), was hypnotically peering at us from the end of a Basswood stick, perhaps wondering when its next meal would arrive.

An advertisement I read in a science education magazine in 1960 told of Praying Mantis egg cases for sale. Soon I had several placed inside one of our terrariums in my general science room.

This gravid (heavy with eggs) female European Praying Mantis, beneficial and harmless to humans, poses on Roy's hand as though in prayer. They are gradually becoming more common in Wisconsin. Her spiny, vice-like forearms serve as formidable weapons in the capture of insects of various sizes—virtually anything that moves and comes within striking range.

Surely I had many doubting thomases in my classes hopelessly staring into the terrarium at school, day after day, to see the lifeless and hopeless plastic foam-like mantis egg cases.

Then one warm late spring morning there came a "WHOOPEE!" from a few of the students that must have carried throughout most of the junior high school in Wisconsin Rapids. The case was full of incredibly tiny baby Praying Mantises. Finally the eggs had hatched. The students believed me, and my spirits soared.

It wasn't long before the youngsters realized by their careful observing that some of the small insects were eating their own kind. "They're cannibalistic! What should we do?"

One by one the students took their own pet praying mantis home where they would attempt to raise it. How eagerly the quarter-inch-long creatures accepted small bits of raw meat dangled in front of them on a piece of thread. Flies and other small insects, dropped into the glass case, quickly disappeared.

Our lone surviving mantis at school grew rapidly and became quite the pal to everyone. "IT" was a terror to other insects but perfectly harmless to humans. In retrospect this may have been one of the most important lessons my 140 science students learned that year. How thrilled I was to watch what at first were very squeamish students eventually allow the fearsome looking insect to crawl up their arm or perch on their shoulder or the tip of an outstretched finger.

What really triggered my initial interest in the Praying Mantis was a fascinating chapter, "Dinah Was A Mantis" that I read in Edwin Way Teale's exciting book, *Near Horizons, the Story of an Insect Garden,* published by Robert Hale Limited (London) in 1947.

Following our highly successful adventure with the Praying Mantis, I wrote a letter to Mr. Teale describing in detail the fun and learning that, in a way, he had helped to promote. Naturally I had hoped to receive a reply from the author but never did. Later, after reading most of the great books on nature he wrote, I came to realize what an unusually busy person he was.

Had the movie, "ET," been produced when my students and I were having the times of our lives with the pet mantis, perhaps they too would have nicknamed it "ET" as we have done today with ours, 28 years later. The triangular-shaped head and large compound eyes of the Praying Mantis immediately reminded us of the lovable ET of movie fame.

Only one species of mantid, of the 1,800 worldwide, is native to the United States, the Carolina Mantid. The only mantids fairly common in parts of the northern states are two introduced species, the European Mantid, about two inches long, and the Chinese Mantid, around four inches long.

The identifying feature of our European Mantid is the black-ringed whitish spot beneath both of its fore coxae, those parts of the front legs nearest the thorax. These legs are heavily armored with spines and teeth and can move with great speed to capture prey. These include many kinds of insects regarded by people to be helpful in some cases and harmful in others. The mantids don't choose. They simply eat!

Mantids' very strong mouthparts are capable of biting through the quite hard, plastic-like, chitinous (KITE-i-nus) exoskeletons of insects such as beetles and wasps. The long middle and hind legs give the Praying Mantis the ability to remain motionless for many minutes at a time, its front legs "raised in prayer," as it patiently waits for its prey insects to unsuspectingly crawl or land near the perpetually hungry mantis. Obviously its praying-like attitude is reflected in the *religiosa* species name of the European Mantid.

In light of the Praying Mantis' amazing front leg speed in seizing its prey, the mantis is otherwise a slow-moving insect. The winged adult's flight is short and labored.

What a thing of beauty, to see a mantid slowly turn its head and watch your every movement as though thoroughly captivated. I wonder whether the mantis is the only insect able to turn its head and look over its shoulder like a human. Little wonder it is such as enchanting creature.

And so it was with our ET, like Edwin Way Teale's, Dinah, "Life drifted into death with the calm transition of day passing through twilight into darkness."

Everyone should have at least one pet Praying Mantis in their life, an Emotional Thrill, an Enriching Treat, a form of Educational Therapy at its best, a genuine ET to top them all!

It was Robert Frost, renowned American poet, who described the classical method by which to slice an apple. He said, "You never cut an apple from the top of the stem to the bottom. You cut it sideways. When you do it that way it makes the apple easier to eat and it reduces waste. And you see the star shape of the seed containers."

The Cosmopolitan Fruit

Judging by the millions of apple trees in the United States, the leading apple-growing country in the world, and the fact that the apple is the cosmopolitan fruit of all fruits, it's surprising that this great favorite is not native to the US. They are native to southwestern Asia and adjacent Europe. However, I would be the last to tell anyone that the apple pie is not the all-American dessert!

The history of some of the names of apples would be interesting to pursue, such as Newton Pippin, Northern Spy, Golden Russet, Talman Sweet, Baldwin, Winesap, Rome Beauty, Tompkins King, Johnathon, McIntosh and Black Gilliflower.

It has been proven beyond a doubt that the world's best-known fruit tree of temperate climates is the apple. Approximately 700 million bushels are produced annually in this zone, around 100 million in the United States alone.

One could accurately describe this versatile food as America's number-one, five-star fruit. It was Robert Frost, great American poet, who alerted me to an often-overlooked fact. His method was to slice apples in an unorthodox poetic manner. He said, "You never cut an apple from the top of the stem to the bottom. You cut it sideways. When you do it that way it makes the apple easier to eat and it reduces waste. And you see the star shape of the seed containers."

Botanically an apple is called a pome, a fleshy fruit without a stone. Hawthornes, Serviceberries, Pears and Quinces are also pomes. Each fruit has a thin, bony, plastic-like inner wall called the ovary wall, producing the tiny chambers which enclose the seeds. A cross-section of these chambers is a striking five-pointed star.

I tried the "Frost On the apple" method and it works. The last thing I did with each round slice was to pop the star-shaped center portion into my mouth and carefully munch on the remaining pulp. Now all I had left were the thin bony sections of the carpels. Eleven seeds, a very tiny pile of carpel sections, and the stem were all that remained from the juicy perfumed Cortland. Never again will I slice an apple from top to bottom!

As boys, to us an apple was a "YUBL-ko," the phonetic spelling for the Czechoslovakian word for apple, "jablko," a lip-smacking sound in itself. Jablka (YUBL-ka) is plural for apple. Little did we realize our expertise in locating good jablka. One apple tree, long overlooked by whoever owned it, grew near our favorite swimming beach just south of the Leyse Aluminum Factory in Kewaunee. By August the green apples were just right for eating, sour as they were. But what a lift they would give us in our strenuous play and swimming. I doubt that any apples ever reached maturity on that tree during our boyhood.

Some friends taught me a good sautéed apple recipe when I was still a bachelor, destitute of cooking know-how. Cut about two pounds of apples into eighths removing the cores but leaving the skins on. This amount should just about fill your skillet. Pour in about one-half to three-fourths cup brown sugar and one-half cup sweet wine, such as red rosé wine. Add one-half teaspoon nutmeg and two tablespoons butter. Cover skillet and cook until apples are fairly soft. Remove cover and cook until liquid is thick, then eat as you smack your lips after every mouthful! By all means leave the skins on when you stew your apples. The color of the final product will be improved and the flavor greatly enhanced because it is said that the best flavor is directly beneath the skin.

As a boy, many winter nights were spent with my folks, three brothers and sister eating homemade popcorn topped off with our favorites, Golden Delicious apples, as we listened to "Fibber McGee and Molly" or some other radio program. And many a time I climbed one of the McIntosh apple trees in our backyard at noon in fall to fetch a couple of delectable tree-ripened "Macs" to be eaten during afternoon school recess.

I fondly remember how expertly my Grandma Skala could peel an apple in one long continuous ribbon. Then she'd tell us to throw the peel over our shoulder. The letter formed as it fell to the floor would be that of the girl we would marry some day. The first one I tossed must have formed a "C," the apple of my eye! Chances are the apples she was peeling for pie or sauce came from a Duchess of Oldenburg tree growing on the west side of their home.

Many a lucky farm child was unknowingly exposed to some wonderful apple orchard ornithology in the family's organically-grown, unsprayed orchard. There one might find the nesting sites of the Eastern Kingbird, American Robin, American Goldfinch, Baltimore Oriole, Eastern Bluebird, Downy Woodpecker, Black-capped Chickadee and others. I have fond reminiscences of birding there and especially the early-ripening green "cooking" (and eating!) apple tree, most likely one of the "transparents," that grew at the farm on the south side of the granary overlooking the Opicka Valley and the Kewaunee River southeast of Casco.

One well-known tree grew at the west end of Anton Kieweg's garden in Kewaunee, fortunately right across the hedge from our Saturday morning football "stadium" at Kieweg's Park. That tree was a late October or early November tree as I recall. Those deep red apples seemed to improve in taste after they were slightly frozen, and we just couldn't stand to see those delectable fruits go to waste. More than once we had to carry them in our pockets for a while until they thawed enough to be eaten.

Henry David Thoreau preferred to eat his apples "with a sauce of sharp November Air" too. He would fill both front pockets with apples and then methodically eat one from the left pocket, then the right, so he would keep in good balance as he walked.

Count yourselves lucky to be living in excellent apple country where words such as tang, crispness, perfume, hardiness, ambrosial and delectable are most often used to describe America's five-star fruit, the "YUBL-ko!"

Woody Recyclers

Even though the mushroom season came upon us painfully slowly this fall due to the hot dry summer, eventually the rains arrived bringing out some of the choicest of edibles. In fact it was downright pleasurable introducing several friends to an old-time favorite, the Honey Cap, *Armillariella mellea.* (am-mi-lair-ee-EL-la MEL-lee-a). Did Charlotte's delectable mushroom soup ever disappear amid grins and sighs of deep satisfaction!

We like to think that perhaps the inch and a half of rain that fell during the past two days may bring about a resurgence of good mushrooms. At least we'll be out looking for them this week-end. Should our enjoyable search for them not be productive, surely there will be a host of interesting woody fungi to enjoy and perhaps to photograph.

The more easily recognized woody fungi I have in mind go by a host of common names including Bracket Fungus, Shelf Fungus, Turkey-tail Fungus, Rainbow Conk and the Horse's Hoof Fungus. Most often they are tough and woody, in fact more woody than the very wood upon which they are growing. For the most part they are inedible simply because of their hardness. Reports from England tell that the Birch Polypore was used as a razor strop during the middle 1800's. Another woody fungus, the Thick-walled Maze Polypore, was used as a currycomb for horses with tender skins.

These woody fungi belong to a group called polypores, meaning many-pored. The tube layer which lines the underside of the cap appears to consist of an incredible number of tiny pinholes, some so small that they have to be seen with a hand lens. These are the tubes containing the spores.

You may have heard of the phrase, "There's a fungus among us." Here there are two woody fungi that are growing in a somewhat peculiar arrangement. In this case, the large, semicircular "Shelf Fungus" originally grew on the upright Paper Birch. Upon falling to the ground and being placed in a vertical position, as pictured here, two small woody fungi, their spore-containing pores properly facing downward, began growing along the edge of the rim of the still-alive Shelf Fungus.

The family group to which these polypores belong is the *Polyporaceae* (po-lip-o-RAY-see-ee). What's so amazing about polypores is that they are *the* major group of absolutely indispensable wood-rotting fungi growing in a healthy woods. This will come as a surprise to those people who consider fungi to be damaging to trees.

Even though there are some extremely detrimental fungi to trees, including our great favorite, the Honey Cap, most fungi are actually very important. Through the process of decay, they prevent build-up of forest debris thereby reducing the chances of fire and also providing vital open spaces for the growth of new trees. It is through decomposition that they also contribute toward the build-up of the blanket of humus on the ground which adds protection to tree roots, slows down water runoff and, later, integrates with mineral soil aiding in seed germination and the growth of trees.

In the process of disintegration of dead materials, some of the carbon in them is changed to carbon dioxide, so vital to the growth of green plants, which in turn give off oxygen so critically important to living beings such as you and me!

We simply could not have forests today without the existence of fungi. Furthermore, most tree roots are dependent upon the mycelium (my-SEE-lee-um) of mushrooms in obtaining various nutrients from the soil that cannot be obtained by the trees' roots themselves.

It is often the huge, shelf-like, woody fungus, the so-called Artist's Conk, *Ganoderma applanatum,* (gan-o-DER-ma ap-pla-NAY-tum) that draws so much attention to the hiker. It is not uncommon to find them having the diameter of a bushel basket. The white surface below turns brown when scratched, hence the name Artist's Conk. With care one can make quite a delicate sketch which, when dry, will remain in this condition indefinitely. However, due to the great importance of these fungi, I recommend that they be left intact where they grow, thereby allowing their spores to be spread naturally.

A favorite bracket fungus of ours is the Hemlock Polypore, *Ganoderma tsugae,* (gan-o-DER-ma SOO-gee). *Tsugae* is the genus of hemlocks. The top of this elegant fungus is a rich mahogany that appears to have been varnished yet is perfectly dry to the touch. This indeed may be the woody fungus referred to as the varnished conk. It usually is found on the fallen rotting trunks of hemlock trees.

One of the so-called true tinder polypores is the Horse's Hoof Fungus, *Fomes fomentarius.* Fomes is pronounced FOE-meez. What a striking similarity they have to horse's hooves. Frequently they grow on the trunks of dying or dead hardwoods, especially birch and beech. Years ago, before the advent of matches, chunks of this fungus were soaked in a saltpeter solution, dried, then used in place of matches in some manner or other.

One of the most easily recognized polypores is the Birch Conk, *Piptoporus betulinus,* pronounced pip-toe-PORE-us bet-u-LINE-us. Betula is the genus of the birch. These smooth, roundish, light-colored, hoof-like fungi grow only on dead or dying birches and are quite beautiful not only to look at but also to touch.

One of the most fascinating of all woody fungi is the Turkey-tail or Partridge-tail fungus, *Trametes versicolor.* Trametes is pronounced tra-ME-teez. One might also call it the many-colored polypore. What a lovely array of earthy colors are included on a rotting stump literally covered by these thin, leathery, velvety little shelves. White, gray, tan, brown, yellowish-buff, black and even green from a thin coating of algae are included in multi-colored zones on the turkey tails.

As so often happens, objects of great beauty in nature are also of tremendous value. Such is the case with the intriguing variety of woody polypores. Some have good reason to fan their little "turkey tails" in proud pomposity!

Seeds Of Life

A big, fluffy, parachuting Milkweed seed blew against the back of my neck a few days ago startling me as I worked in the garden. With so many wood wasps buzzing around the south side of the garden shed in the sunshine I instinctively thought that one of them had landed on my neck rather than the silky white, wind-blown seed.

As much as a lot of people do not favor the competition of Milkweed plants in their fields, gardens, or on their lawns, we carefully tend the small patches of them that grow north of our garden and along the west side of our house. Not only do we enjoy the large clusters of small, fragrant, lavender flowers that attract a host of various insects, but we also hope that some female Monarch butterflies will lay their eggs on one or more of the plants.

We watched two Monarch caterpillars mature during the summer, one in each of the two milkweed patches, and also were fortunate to locate and photograph one of the chrysalises that had been fastened to the upper edge of our air conditioner near some of the plants. Eventually an adult female emerged and also was captured on film as she hung while her wings expanded and dried.

There are literally thousands of ways one can relate to seeds during the fall season, especially now that nearly all of the vegetables have been harvested. The very first seeds I can recall planting were grass seeds, a simple "window sill" project when I was in the fourth grade. Each of us brought two similar drinking glasses from home, and planted in one of the glasses some grass seeds in soil, both provided by our teacher, Helen Bruemmer. We watered them and placed the other glass on top of the "garden." How exciting it was to see the seeds grow in our miniature terrariums— and that's about all I remember of that project.

How well I recall one of my first years of teaching and of telling my students to bring interesting things they had found in nature to school so we might study them in our science classes. One of the students brought an entire shopping bag full of milk-weed pods. Unfortunately I put the bag of pods in one of the cupboards and forgot about them. Several weeks later we went to retrieve them and were astounded by the thousands of fluffy, parachuted seeds that had dried and, because the seed pods had fully split open, were now being wafted by air currents throughout the classroom – a virtual "snow-storm!"

I was in sixth grade the year World War II broke out in 1941 and I can recall receiving some zucchini squash seeds at school the following spring with which to start our so-called "Victory Garden" at home. That was the first time we had ever heard of this squash, little realizing that it had the reputation of producing more edible weight of vegetable per seed than any other seeds planted. My parents were avid vegetable and flower gardeners for as long as I can remember, so the zucchini plants were merely a supplement to their already huge garden.

Right about now my Dad would have been making up his several huge bouquets or center-pieces using colorful stems of three of his favorite fall plants, Silver Dollars, Bittersweet and Chinese Lanterns, all of which he grew at our home. It was in the border of the north garden where he grew the ubiquitous Silver Dollars, *Lunaria annua,* also called the Money Plant and Honesty. The parchment discs, remaining where the outer coverings had been slipped from each side, brought about the name of Silver Dollars. Collecting these fascinating seed pods was bound to release some of the tiny seeds which, in turn, fell to the ground and germinated the following spring. Being biennials it took two years for the flowers and seeds to develop.

Charlotte and I have purchased some Amish heirloom seeds of the delicious "Brandywine" tomato for several years and think this is one of the finest tasting of all tomatoes. Most seed catalogs carry them at present.

One of these years we plan to put more effort into saving some of our own seeds to be planted the following spring. Seeds that we have collected from our plants and have grown the following year are from Purple Coneflowers and the Mexican Sunflower, *Tithonia.*   Bearing brilliant orange flowers, this colorful sunflower grows to around five feet, responds well to compost and likes quite a bit of sun. Both of these garden flowers were visited by hundreds of butterflies this past summer. The *Tithonias* are very easy to grow — one of our favorites.

Recently we have been noticing many small songbirds along roadsides as we drove through the countryside. Juncos, White-throated and Tree Sparrows, and Yellow-rumped Warblers were four species that we could identify. Our guess is that these birds are continually attracted to the narrow patch of ground directly adjacent to the blacktop for the multitude of seeds to be found there. Another guess is that the most abundant seeds are those of the Ragweed. Many species of birds are known to consume these relatively large seeds.

Ragweed invariably grows the best on this narrow band of ground due to the constant disturbance brought about by automobile tires and especially the scraping of snowplow blades in winter. Most weeds, including Ragweed, thrive in disturbed ground, where the competition from other plants is the least and where they can get full sunlight.

There is another seed we will always remember during this season when Ruffed Grouse are known to perform their unusual "crazy" flights. No one really knows why this occurs. Several years ago we were driving along a narrow highway that wound its way through a swamp and where the vegetation grew quite close to the edge of the road.

Without warning, a Ruffed Grouse flew out of the swampy woods directly into the path of our oncoming car. Unfortunately we were unable to avoid the collision, but fortunately the bird didn't come through our windshield. Rather it hit our car at the very top of our left headlight, then smacked into the upper left side of our windshield and, in so doing, splattered most of the glass with hundreds of yellow, disc-shaped seeds of the Highbush Cranberry fruits it had recently been eating.

Seeds are minute, but they contain the very germs of the wonderful green mantle of our planet. Our bodies, along with those of our countless partners in nature, could not survive without seeds. How small but important they are to our very existence!

This miniature owl that tips the scales at about four and one-third ounces is also one of the most secretive and seldom seen. The Saw-whet Owl was named because its call resembles the sound a person might produce when filing the teeth of a hand saw, a very raspy, screechy sound. One look at its eyes and you may agree that they appear proportionately large for the size of the head. Perhaps this is due to the rather small size of the bird's facial discs, those parabolically-shaped "saucers" surrounding the eyes whose function it is to gather sounds and concentrate them in the vicinity of the ear openings.

Little Wise Guy

There is a small bird, shorter than an American Robin, that is silently heading south through some of the thickets and swamps of eastern Wisconsin during the night. A lot of birdwatchers would give their eye-teeth to get a glimpse of one of these seldom-seen raptors, smallest of the lot to nest in this state, the Saw-whet Owl.

People who live near Tamarack bogs, heavy groves of Northern White Cedars or swampy Aspen and Alder tangles stand the best chance of lucking onto one of these miniature owls, chocolate-brown above with fine streaks, white below with rather broad brown vertical stripes.

This sixth smallest of all North American owls goes by other names in the North such as Acadian Owl, Kirtland's Owl, Sparrow Owl and White-fronted Owl. One French-Canadian name, "La Chouette Des Granges De L'est," means the little night owl.

Perhaps if its song were more owl-like, such as the Great-horned Owl's "whoWHOOO – who who who," or the Barred Owl's "WHO COOKS FOR YOU — WHO COOKS FOR YOUall," more people who watch and listen outdoors at night would get to know this beautiful creature. Whether the Saw-whet is making its monotone, short, whistled "WHOOK - WHOOK - WHOOK" or its "scratchy" saw-sharpening-like song, "SWEEaww – SWEEaww – SWEEaww," the tone is generally near middle C or slightly higher. Few people, upon hearing this nighttime music, would ever guess it is coming from a tiny owl. If you can imagine whetting, or sharpening, a saw using a file, the resulting raspy sound somewhat resembles this tiny owl's song.

Up until around a dozen years ago there was a lot of guesswork by the experts regarding the distribution and numbers of Saw-whet Owls in this region. Trapping and banding a small number of them after dark began to shed some light on the matter.

However, it wasn't until the fall of 1987 when our friend, Tom Erdman, began using tape-recorded songs of these owls that a larger number were lured into his mist net traps after dark to be captured, banded, studied and released. That year a total of 526 Saw-whets were banded by Tom.

About ten separate pieces of data are gathered and recorded for each Saw-whet captured. The obvious data are the bird's weight, length of outer primary wing-feathers and length of tail. Less suspected data include the molting condition of flight feathers and the color of the iris. Even the exact location of each bird's capture, the specific net and in which "shelf" of that net the bird was trapped, are also recorded.

One look at this beautiful little creature makes it difficult to realize that there are five smaller species of owls in North America, the Whiskered, Flammulated, Ferruginous Pygmy, Northern Pygmy, and the smallest, the Whitney's Elf Owl weighing in at a mere nine-tenths of one ounce! Average weight of a Saw-whet is 4.3 ounces. Compare this to the heaviest of all North American owls, the Snowy Owl that tips the scales at 58 ounces on the average. Close behind is the Great-horned at 53.3 ounces. The quite abundant "Hoot Owl" of Northeastern Wisconsin, the Barred Owl, weighs about 16 ounces.

Every time I look at a Saw-whet Owl I get the feeling that its eyes are disproportionately large for the size of its head.   Perhaps this is due to the rather small size of the bird's facial discs, those parabolically-shaped "saucers" surrounding the eyes whose function it is to gather sounds and concentrate them in the vicinity of the ear openings.

What incredibly acute hearing these little birds of the night have. Upon examination, you will find that their ear-cavities are comparatively very large as well as asymmetrical in size, shape and placement. This makes the head, and especially the skull of many Saw-whets, appear somewhat lopsided or distorted.

This owl's reply to our examination would be, "All the better to hear you with!" Indeed, this little raptor's sensitive hearing easily helps it to pinpoint the movement of animals such as mice, voles, rats, Red Squirrels, bats and frogs. Mice and frogs constitute a large proportion of its food.

Studies indicate that the Saw-whet can eat double its weight in prey in one night. Obviously it must possess very rapid digestive processes.

For those of you with adventure in your blood, obtain some bird records or tapes and learn the mellow songs of the Saw-whet Owl. Come early spring, head for some swamp or Alder thicket and begin listening. Chances of hearing the Saw-whets are a lot better than you may think. You'll return home refreshed and all the wiser, or so the owls would say!

December

White-Tailed Moochers

Everyone knows how children (and a few adults) relish chocolate and ice cream. Perhaps the two most favorite foods of the White-tailed Deer are sweet corn and apples. Little wonder there were plenty of deer tracks for several fall seasons in our sweet corn patch (before we fenced in our garden) growing right next to an old "sport" of an apple tree loaded with fruit.

Fortunately the apples are wild and wormy and we had planted more sweet corn than we could possibly consume ourselves. Ordinarily I don't become too attached to deer, especially those frequenting the garden, but the six-pointed buck and a doe we often saw were exciting to observe.

Naturally Charlotte and I shudder a little on opening day of deer-hunting season to hear the expected "BLAM BLAM BLAM" of the rifles in the woods to the west of our garden. Surely by now the young buck has most likely been transformed into venison sausage and the lucky hunter is happy with his successful experience.

Let's face it, deer are a public as well as a renewable resource. I like to see them alive and to try to photograph them. To others, deer hunting provides recreation, a challenge, good fellowship, exercise and a chance to enjoy the outdoors, and hopefully provides the hunter with some wholesome meat, a hide, and a trophy to hang on the wall.

Even though the White-tailed Deer is such an over-abundant mammal throughout most of the state it remains a great favorite to watch and to admire. This large healthy doe, living in an area that is off-limits to hunting, her "radar" ears held erect to capture the slightest sound, stands at the precise angle whereby the shadow of her head and neck is cast upon her back.

A fairly recent estimate placed the value of each deer harvested in the United States at about $1,250. Included in the figure were license fees, food, lodging, entertainment, hunting clothes and equipment, travel expenses, lost earnings, and butchering costs.

In 1974 about two million White-tailed Deer were shot in the United States by over eight million hunters. This brings the total value of that year's kill to around $2.5 billion! That's big business if I ever saw it!

Consider too the negative impact from deer such as crop damage, injury and deformation of trees in plantations, destruction of ornamental shrubs (landscaped), flowers and vegetables, and car-deer collisions amounting to somewhat over $100 million annually in the United States and Canada.

The fact that the deer herd in Wisconsin has fluctuated considerably during the past 135 years indicates that people have great influence on their numbers. We affect in many ways the quality and quantity of food the deer will consume. For example there was a great increase in their numbers following the massive timber harvest in this state during the late 1800's. Excellent "edge" containing choice deer food was created by the logging.

The combination of small woodlots, many with evergreens, and the abundance of food provided by the agriculturists today results in optimum conditions for a high deer population. Little by little the state is getting a better handle on the proper management of the deer, and is being looked up to as one of the leaders in this very difficult and challenging profession.

If you think this has been an easy process covering the past 135 years you have another guess coming! One of the very best books describing in part this complicated movement is, *Thinking Like A Mountain: Aldo Leopold and the Evolution of an Ecological Attitude Toward Deer, Wolves and Forests,* written by Susan L. Flader and published in 1974 by the University of Missouri Press. How I would like to see this book become mandatory reading by every deer hunter!

Another book I cherish, a "required reading" text too, is Wallace Byron Grange's, *The Way to Game Abundance.* Grange said, "…it can be infinitely more interesting, more recreational, if the hunter himself has a hand in the production process." He implied in this fascinating book that people are suffering a habitat dilemma, that we need to expand upon our existing wilderness fragments.

How I have enjoyed studying *A Century of Wisconsin Deer,* written by Otis S. Bersing and published in 1956 (second edition in 1966) by the Wisconsin Conservation Dept. Imagine that Outagamie, Brown, Kewaunee, Door, Winnebago and Calumet Counties had no deer seasons for from 41 to 54 years during the period from 1901-1954.

Then dip back to 1851-1858 when any kind of deer could be shot statewide between July 1 and January 31. Deer were reported to be numerous in Door County in 1882. By 1888 a deer scarcity was being reported from the northern counties. They were uncommon in Waupaca County in 1897 and by 1912 there were no deer to be found in Door, Kewaunee, Brown, Outagamie, Winnebago, Calumet, Manitowoc and other counties to the south.

In 1914 there was quite a "war" in the woods to the north during the deer hunt with 24 hunters being killed and 26 injured. It sounds more like a "people" season, or do you suppose that by then the deer were shooting back?

By 1921 the deer were practically wiped out of Wisconsin and in 1924 the estimated gun kill of deer was down to around 7,000 statewide. There was no open season state-wide in 1929, and 20 counties still reported having no deer.

Sixty counties were reporting deer by 1938 when around 33,000 were shot. Gradually their numbers began to climb and by 1942 the deer herd probably reached its peak. The first doe and fawn season brought the total kill in 1943 to 128,300, and up to 168,000 in 1950 when for the first time since 1913 it was legal to shoot deer on Chambers Island in Door County.

The 40's, 50's, and early 60's were "stormy" years especially in northern Wisconsin in terms of the regulating of the hunting season and determining the proper deer harvest. By 1961 the variable quota system had been established and the total picture was beginning to improve. A turning point came especially with the advent of the successful and productive deer-management units, about 100 of them, varying in size from small areas to large tracts including several counties.

To give you an idea of how the number of deer within one county can change, there were no deer in Buffalo County (along the Mississippi River on a line due west of Brown County) in 1929. By 1962 the largest deer kill of 2,465 in the entire state occurred in Buffalo County.

Sit back and relax. Enjoy the deer in whatever way meets your fancy. I will continue to prefer the lithe beauty and grace of live deer and the great challenge of capturing their elegance on film. Hunters will help to maintain at least some semblance of a healthy balance between the deer and the land and its plants. I sympathize with those of you who live in areas that are permanently closed to deer hunting, where these large mammals are literally eating you out of "house and home" as well as being terribly destructive to most native vegetation.

As for us, we have fenced in our garden to protect the vegetables, and eagerly wait for the deer hunt with rifles to end so we can safely venture back into our own woods.

Fragrant Spires

The Ojibwe Indians of this region called this tree "jingo'b pikewa'n-dag," a fir tree that goes up to a peak. They used the pitch for colds and to heal sores, and its pungent fragrance was important in their sweat baths.

People in the northern states, for well over a hundred years, have favored the outdoor fresh-ness and aroma it brings into their homes at Christmas time. It was the only tree my Dad ever brought into our home to be trimmed, the Balsam Fir. What a perfect symbol of a living Christ-mas spirit!

These slender, conical, spire-like trees are native to the Northern Hemisphere and grow from southern Wisconsin (sparingly) to about 62 degrees N. latitude. Seldom do they grow to be more than 12 to 15 inches in diameter and 40 to 50 feet tall. The record in this country is a giant growing in Fairfield, Pennsylvania that measures slightly more than 12 feet in circumference and is 100 feet tall.

Their flowers, small and seldom observed by people, occur in late May and by September the cones are nearly ripe. A heavy seed crop occurs at four to six-year intervals. However, some seeds are produced every year. The two to three-inch-long violet-purple, barrel-like cones sit upright on the higher branches. Their scales overlap and are very tight-fitting. Each encloses two wide-winged seeds. By late summer we begin to find the fresh fir cones along the trails, chewed off the trees and accidentally dropped to the ground by Red Squirrels.

Balsam Fir cones ripen differently than spruce or pine cones, for example. Layer by layer, beginning at the top, the fir cones literally fall apart. The seeds are scattered by the wind as the scales fall to the ground, leaving the central axis of the cone standing upright on the twig and looking for all the world like a birthday cake candle. They will remain on the tree for quite a few years.

The invigorating fragrance of these ideal Christmas trees is looked forward to by millions of people each year. Blisters containing this heady resin occur frequently on the older trees. Re-fined, this pitch, called Canada balsam, was used for many years as a glue to imbed a dried specimen between two pieces of glass, then to be viewed through a microscope. This glue dries to the same purity of refraction as the glass slides. Unfortunately this wonderful glue has been replaced today by synthetic man-made glues.

Both top-view and end-view of twigs of the "double" and "single" Balsam Fir trees are shown, the "double" at the left, the "single" at the right. The two examples were removed from the same tree, the "double" from the sun-drenched top portion of the fir, the "single" from the lower, shaded, northern side of the tree.

Another prime feature of the Balsam Fir can be quickly sensed by running your hand against the grain of the needles in toward the trunk. They're soft and comfortable to the touch. In the first place they're rounded at the tips, but they're also flat. What a pleasure it is to decorate one of these trees.

Surprisingly many people wonder about the difference between a fir and a spruce. Spruces are short-needled, sharply-pointed, and are very spiny to the touch. Remember SPiny, SPruce. Even though beautifully-shaped spruces are quite common, one has to guard against their drying out, thereby becoming messy and extremely flammable when brought indoors.

Consider making the best possible use of your Balsam Fir after it has served as a Christmas tree. Sew a couple of four by six-inch flat cotton bags with a zipper on one long side. Spread several sheets of newspaper on the floor. Cut the branches off your tree within a few inches from the trunk and strip off all the needles. Fill the pillows and zip them shut. Placed on the top backs of the living room sofa and chairs, they will add fragrance to your home year after year.

You may have heard about single versus double Balsam Fir trees. Essentially, single Balsams are shade-grown while double Balsams are sun-grown. The needles of those trees growing in the sun are heated on their tops causing them to dry out slightly and curl upward. This in turn gives this tree more "fullness." The needles of shade-grown Balsams remain quite horizontal, giving these trees a more open shape, not nearly as full as the "double."

People have often asked me, "Isn't it better conservation to use artificial Christmas trees?" My answer is NO! Man-made trees are constructed of precious, non-renewable natural resources. Once they're gone they're gone forever. Trees are a renewable resource. In fact, some states plant and sell more than three million Christmas trees annually. Somewhat over 30 million are distributed each year at this time.

Theodore Roosevelt, during his first years in the White House, tried to set an example for other Americans by not allowing a tree to be cut and used at Christmas time in the nation's Capitol. Friends eventually led him to see the value of trees as a yearly crop, helping many people earn a living. Thinning out stands of evergreens also promoted better growth of other trees. Soil too poor for crops was often satisfactory for growing evergreens. In fact, slower growth brings about the development of denser and more symmetrical Christmas trees.

Evergreen trees that people bring indoors at Christmas time have various desirable features that people like such as retention of needles after the tree is cut, especially when used indoors, compact conical shape, fullness, not too prickly, pleasant green color, enough limb strength to hold ornaments and lights, pliability and fragrance. Few evergreen species possess more of these characteristics than Balsam Firs. No wonder it has ranked as the No. 1 Christmas tree in America for so many years.

"Butterflies" Of Winter

A bird some old timers called the English parrot has finally arrived on the scene. Scientists refer to it as *Coccothraustes vespertinus,* indicating that this bird is a "seed crusher of the evening." There should be no doubt in your mind that this welcome visitor from the north is the Evening Grosbeak.

Our friends, the Delcarsons, reported the first ones from Fish Creek on Thursday, October 26 (1995). By the next day calls were coming from all directions, including as far away as Waupaca, telling of the arrival of the "big-beaks" at their feeders. Apparently a huge wave of the flashy black, white, yellow and olive birds had swept into northeastern Wisconsin overnight.

This "double-decker" platform feeder, shown here with at least two dozen Evening Grosbeaks stuffing their gullets with sunflower seeds, has proven through the years to be our most effective and attractive feeder. The two 16x30-inch wooden platforms are simply separated by three 2 x 4's producing about a two-inch-deep lower platform. This in turn is mounted on a stout post, high enough off the ground to prevent squirrels from jumping on, and is encircled with a metal baffle to prevent any mammal from climbing to the top.

Major Delafield, an agent of the United States for boundaries, first described them in 1823 near the Savannah River northwest of Lake Superior. His notes indicate these trusting birds approached his tent at twilight and that their mournful cries attracted the men's attention. Delafield implied the creatures inhabited the dark swampy areas by day and came out of their hiding during the early evening hours, hence Evening Grosbeaks.

In all likelihood, the major and his men had disturbed the birds on their roosts, thereby bringing forth the unsettled cries. Actually these hardy migrants are most active in the early part of each day.

Their movements in North America are very interesting. They were practically unknown in eastern US up to 1890. By 1911 they were being seen as far south as New York City during the winter. One theory is that their gradual eastward movement may have followed the widespread planting of the Box Elders, *Acer Negundo,* also called Ash-leafed Maple and Manitoba Maple. This member of the maple genus produces winged seeds that are relished by these gluttonous grosbeaks.

The lower mandible of a Western Evening Grosbeak was discovered among the fossils at the famous Rancho La Brea tar pits near Los Angeles. These world famous remains of prehistoric animals are generally dated at about 20,000 years old, indicating that these sturdy birds have been on this continent for a very long time.

Southern migration in fall is obviously related to their search for food. Very few will venture south of the 45th Parallel in some winters. This runs generally from Jacksonport in Door County west to Wausau and beyond. In unusual years their wanderings will take them to Louisiana, Mississippi and Alabama.

Our records indicate that, starting in 1964, we had them at our feeders in Baileys Harbor for at least ten straight years. In fact they were so abundant one winter that we purchased 44 50-pound bags of sunflower seeds that year (over one ton!). There were days when we estimated nearly 300 Evening Grosbeaks in our yard at one time. Bear in mind that other bird species were consuming sunflower seeds too!

Being late nesters they can usually be seen at backyard feeders easily into late April and occasionally into the last week of May. They nest sparingly in northern Wisconsin. My field records indicate observing several pair near Champion, Michigan in July of 1960. I saw a pair in northern Door County, at the Mud Lake Wildlife Area, on July 23, 1971.

The outward conspicuousness of the white, yellow, olive and black males would lead you to think that Mother Nature went astray in making them such easy "stand-outs" for their predators. Actually the bold color pattern helps them to blend very well with the bright splashes of lichens growing on most of the trees in their summer range, the northern spruce forest.

Members of the large group of finches, including Evening Grosbeaks, Pine Grosbeaks and American Goldfinches, have several obvious characteristics. They are tree-dwellers of the forest or its edges; they sing during flight, are highly sociable and do not exhibit strong migratory tendencies. They move southward irregularly in winter, and travel in well-knit flocks.

The extraordinarily heavy, yellowish-white cone-shaped beak marks the vociferous Evening Grosbeaks well. Not only does it serve them in opening sunflower seeds, cracking cherry pits and snipping off the unwanted wings of the maple seeds, it also brings about the utmost respect from bird banders who have occasion to handle them. My fingers have been "bloodied up" by them more than once in past years.   I compared their bite with someone grabbing hold of your finger with a pair of sharp pliers and squeezing until it bled.

Dr. Fran Hamerstrom, noted authority and handler of eagles, hawks and owls, was overheard on one occasion, when finding a grosbeak caught in her trapping nets, to say, "Oh, not another one of THOSE things!" According to her she would have much rather handled large hawks than grosbeaks!

To an inventor these strong creatures would stand out as wonderfully designed winter birds. They are unusually well-insulated having a thick layer of down beneath their feathers. Short legs enable these grosbeaks to easily keep them warm while roosting. In examining their feet you will discover that the undersides are padded with tiny, horny, callused knobs. This feature helps them to cling to icy branches.

Our friend, Emma Toft, compared a wintering flock of Evening Grosbeaks to a tree full of yellow flowers or Tiger Swallowtail butterflies. Others have claimed they were eating them out of house and home but that the expense of feeding them was well worth it.

To us they extend the beauty and music in winter that is provided for us in summer by their cousins, the Rose-breasted Grosbeaks. Welcome back daytime "evening" friends!

The Christmas Bird

If the label "Christmas Bird" were to be given to any one species of bird in a predominantly evergreen-tree backyard it would be the Cardinal. One male in his fiery brilliance seems to make the scene come alive. And the female, too, wearing her usual glob of orange-red "lipstick," stands out beautifully against the deep green spruces and pines.

John James Audubon summed it up perfectly when he said, "In richness of plumage, elegance of motion, and strength of song, this species surpasses all its kindred in the United States."

How well I recall my first sighting of a male Cardinal during my army days at Fort Sill, Oklahoma in the spring of 1954. We had arrived early at a rendezvous point on the vast artillery firing range and found ourselves with an hour of free time as we waited for the crew towing the huge atomic cannons to catch up with us. "Hurry up and wait," was our motto!

Having become thoroughly conditioned to finding black oil sunflower seeds at our double-decker platform feeder, this female cardinal, upon arriving in the early morning to find the feeder "wrapped" in soft fluffy snow, knew exactly where and how to get at the life-sustaining seeds. In she went and out she came, with one seed at a time, until she had her fill.

The morning was warm and pleasant and the quiet woods inviting, so I grabbed a pair of binoculars from the supply box and set out to explore the nearby woods. Those moments of quiet were so precious to me then, for soon the absolute loudest of all artillery pieces, the 216 millimeter (bore size) atomic cannons would be blasting away while we trained diligently to kill people. Unknown to nearly all of us in our crew, the time would arrive in the future whereby our hearing would be quite severely damaged.

A shrill human-like whistle, "CHEEer, CHEEer, CHEEer," startled me and immediately the challenge was on. That musical beacon was so perfect that one could hardly miss. The song was one I had never heard before, adding greatly to the excitement. Suddenly there he was in all his scarlet finery and not in the least concerned with my presence, my very first Cardinal!

It was not until the late 1950's that I saw my first Cardinal in my hometown of Kewaunee. About that time I discovered a small printed notice tucked into an old bird book I had purchased at Paul's Used Book Store in Madison, the city in which I was teaching at the time. The notice was printed in about 1903 and sent to various birdwatchers throughout Wisconsin asking them to assist in a winter bird survey. Special mention was directed to those living in the southern counties of the state, to be on the watch for Cardinal grosbeaks (as they were referred to then), because a few had been seen near Lake Geneva.

Apparently their range was just beginning to include Wisconsin. According to old records, Cardinals were only casually seen north of the Ohio River Valley by 1886. Today they are common nesters throughout most of Wisconsin and into southern Ontario. Surely a combination of factors has brought about their range expansion. The dominant breeding Cardinals in spring drive other Cardinals to different areas. Then too, Cardinals are known to group together and do some wandering in winter, expanding their breeding range in the process.

Shrikes, hawks, feral cats and too much human activity are known to drive these shy birds to different more protected environments. Chances are they are encouraged to remain in certain habitats by the proper cover and the food set out for them by people. Come spring, some of those birds will nest nearby and continue to bring their young to also feed on the handouts.

Those of you who live near the edges of woods or thickets where tangles of small trees, shrubs and vines occur will very likely see Cardinals. Put sunflower seeds out for the birds and the "Redbirds" will surely find them. These regular customers will undoubtedly number among your favorites.

When Charlotte and I lived at the Ridges Sanctuary, where superb Cardinal habitat existed practically up to our back door, we soon came to enjoy the early morning and evening periods which we labeled "Cardinal time." Often we would sit quietly at the kitchen table within several feet from where the Cardinals came to feed. Charlotte would count the males while I counted the females. Our high number one evening in November of 1975 was 12 males and 8 females, counted at one instant.

Generally by late fall the young will have molted and by winter, in their new plumage, will look just like the adults. The soft olive-gray feather-edges will wear off by spring and the males will be adorned in their most aristocratic elegance, the reddest of the Cardinal reds.

One of their classy characteristics, of which we are especially fond, is their tail-bobbing and flitting, with a slight side-to-side twisting motion, as they fly away. Their distinctive "chip-chip-chip" call notes, somewhat metallic in quality, are easy for most people to hear. Although both sexes are known to sing, indistinguishable from one another according to some experts, I like to think of the brilliant male, perched high in a nearby maple tree in early spring, sounding off with his crystal-clear "CHEEer, CHEEer, CHEEer" or his "WHITyear, WHITyear, WHITyear" songs.

Cardinals, spring songs? Here Christmas hasn't even arrived and spring is already on my mind! Oh well, enjoy the winter holidays with all your Cardinals.

Commune With Nature

I thought deeply about the first verse of one of my favorite poems by Robert Frost, "Stopping By Woods On a Snowy Evening," as I too watched one of the finest woods I know of in this area slowly, mystically and silently receive its first snowy blanket of the season.

Rightfully, I should thank the people who own and have so lovingly preserved this small tract of forest – for doing what they have, for providing many of the native plants, especially the magnificent Sugar Maples and Eastern Hemlocks, a place where they can grow and do what they do best.

Many people, myself included, believe that Henry David Thoreau had the right idea when he said, "the order of things should be somewhat reversed; the seventh day should be man's day of toil…and the other six his Sabbath of the affections and the soul – in which to range this wide spread garden and drink in the soft sublime revelations of nature…"

Thoreau's short life was geared to wholeness and being, not the fulfillment of specialization. If there was anything he particularly despised, it was "getting and spending." Apparently it was this philosophy that led him, through daily observation of people, to state that, "the mass of men lead lives of quiet desperation." Throughout life he urged people to economize and to simplify. What an example of living in harmony with nature he set for the world to follow!

In this day when people are finally being impressed (and stunned) with the fact that fossil fuels will not last for too many more years, the teachings of Thoreau begin to hit home. He tried desperately to impress people with the idea that "most luxuries, and many of the so-called comforts of life are not only not indispensable but positive hindrances to the elevation of mankind. Our life is frittered away by detail…simplify, simplify."

Some of these thoughts of Thoreau gently simmered deep inside me as a group of us friends sat around a table trying to come to grips with the changes in our society, ways in which they might be dealt with, and lastly and most importantly, how they should help to positively alter and influence our lives.

There appeared to be general agreement on the need to be more conservative in our use of natural resources – reduce, reuse, recycle. And yet our discussion was obviously not leading toward individuals making hard and fast commitments on the spot. It's one thing to talk about a pledge, and another thing to perform it, to hold to it.

The idea of the United States leading toward being more of a leisure-time society was discussed. Most likely it is the shortage of some natural resources, resulting in quite a few thousands of people being laid off from work, that led to this idea.

Might the day arrive when, in order for there to be some work available for those who must be wage earners, that people will have to get along with working fewer hours per week and earning less money? This will mean that there will be more and more leisure time on people's hands.

Couple this with a decreasing amount of available gasoline and oil, for example, and you begin to get the picture. People are simply going to have to resort to types of recreation that will keep them closer to home. As I have emphasized in about 1740 nature essays written to date, "look to nature for the best of recreation."

I can't think of a better seasonally related topic to promote at this point than cross country skiing. Call it ski touring if you wish. We have waited for it as eagerly as most youngsters wait for Christmas vacation and Christmas. The reasons are many. As a sport it offers excellent exercise but at the same time is very safe and easy. It is amazingly inexpensive and one doesn't need much snow. The beautiful part is that you can ski almost anywhere outdoors, setting your own pace as you do so. As an added benefit this sport is delightfully quiet and exhilarating.

Ski "back in" somewhere, stop in your tracks, then discover what it is like for the woods to be quiet. What a way to discover the regions of your own inner world and to commune with nature.

The more you do it the more you will realize that you are a birdwatcher, that trees and lichens and other forms in the natural world are taking on so much more meaning. Even the sky and the exciting formation of clouds will come alive.

And then the day arrives when you've come to feel quite proficient on your skis and you pause at the end of a pleasurable and inspirational outing, look up toward the sky and realize that this is the only earth we shall have – ever! Slow down, simplify, "drink in the soft sublime revelations of nature," and stop to watch the woods fill up with snow!

This ice-clad shore-line and snow-decorated landscape reflect the quiet beauty of winter at her finest. This is the type of quiet solitude that reflects peace and harmony, a scene that one would hope will remain intact for generation after generation to love and to cherish. Locate similar natural areas in your home area and, with the help of many friends, work to preserve them forever. From the bottom of my heart I say, *"KEEP DOOR COUNTY WILD!"*

Index

A

A Century of Wisconsin Deer 237
accipiter 16
Acer Negundo 244
Acorn, Red-Oak **203**
Actaea 178
Actaea neglecta 178
Actaea pachypoda 178
Actaea rubra 178
Acutiloba 93
Age of Ferns 119
Alabama 93, 244
Alaska 93, 200
Alder 229
Algoma 30
Algonquin Nation 199
Amanita 186
America 66
American 241
American Heritage Dictionary 200
An Indian Summer 26
Anemone 95
Anemone, Wood 92
Anne, Queen 155, 156
Antarctica 46
Apple **216**, 218
apple 217
Appleton - Foreword
Appleton Post-Crescent - Intro
Appleton, Wisconsin 50
Arborvitae 35, 99, **195**
Arctic 35, 54
Arctic Circle 200
Arctic Ocean 136
Argentina 136
Armillariella mellea 220
Arora, David 183

Asia 179, 200, 217
Aspen 229
Aspen, Large-toothed 39
Aspen, Quaking 39, 181
Audubon, John James 246

B

Badger 113
Baileys Harbor 4, 54, 161, 244
Baileys Harbor Bay **211**
Baileys Harbor Cemetery 46
Balm of Gilead 38, 39, 41
Baneberry 95
Baneberry, Red 178
Baneberry, White 176
Bartlett, John 44
Basalt 46, 47
Basswood 17, 20, 52, 78, 132, **133**, 134,
    135, 193
Bastwood 134
Bear, Black 202
Bear's Rump Island 196
Beaufort wind symbol 7
Bee Balm 118
Bee, Honey 132
Beech, American 67, **87**, 96, 102
Beech, Blue 49
Beecher, Rev. Henry Ward 57
Beetle, June 114
Belgium 153
Bellwort 84, 88, 92
Bentley, Wilson Alwyn
    4, 5, 30, 31, 33, 34
Berlin, Germany 135
Bersing, Otis S. 237
Besserdich, Enid 30
Betula 223

Betula papyrifera 28
Birch, Paper 26, **27**, 67, 102
Birches 29, 30
Bishop's Cap 93
Bittersweet 226
Black Forest 190
Black-eyed Susan 136
Blackbird, Red-winged 58, 115
Bloodroot 84, 88, 89, 91, 92
Blueberry 121, 205
Bluebird, Eastern 219
Bog Laurel 121
Bog Rosemary 121
Borer, Bronze Birch 29
Borkin, Susan 139
Brower, Dr. Lincoln 139
Brown County 73, 237, 238
Bruce Peninsula 196
Bruemmer, Helen 224
Brush Pile & Roy **11**
Buddleia 138
Buffalo County 238
Buffalo, New York Museum of Science 33
Buffaloberry, Canada 38, 83
Bunting, Indigo 88
Bunting, Snow 8
Burlington, Vermont 33
Burns, Robert 88
Buteo 17
Buttercup 95
Butterflies and Moths 126
Butterfly, Anglewing 62, 83, 179
Butterfly, Baltimore Checkerspot **180**
Butterfly Bush 138
Butterfly, Camberwell Beauty 62
Butterfly, Comma 24, **60**, 62, 83
Butterfly, Compton's Tortoise-shell 179
Butterfly, Dorcas Copper 135
Butterfly, Eyed Brown 136

Butterfly, Hairstreak 62
Butterfly, Little Wood Satyr 136
Butterfly, Milbert's Tortoise-shell
    24, 62, 83, 136, 179
Butterfly, Monarch 62, 63, 139, 224
Butterfly, Mourning Cloak 22, 61, 62, 63,
    83, 138, 179, **180**, 181, 182
Butterfly, Northern Pearly Eye **137**
Butterfly, Painted Lady 24, 83, 179
Butterfly, Pearl Crescent Spot 136
Butterfly, Pearly Eye 136
Butterfly, Red Admiral 62, 179
Butterfly, Satyr 136
Butterfly, Small Tortoise Shell 138
Butterfly, Tiger Swallowtail 246
Butterfly, Viceroy 62
Butterfly, White Admiral 62

C

Calumet County 237
Calvatia gigantea 183, 185
Camberwell Beauty 61
Camberwell, England 61
Cambridge, England 135
Camp Crowder, Missouri 159
Canada
    29, 41, 100, 124, 136, 161, 201
Canada Balsam 239
Canadian Research Centre for Anthropol-
    ogy 33
Caraway 153
Carboniferous Period 119
Cardinal 246, 248, 249
Cardinal, female **247**
Casco 219
Cat, House 113
Cattail Marsh **189**
Cave Point **1**
Cedar, Northern White
    82, 173, 174, 194, **195**, 196, 197, 229
Cedar, Western Red 196
Central America 162
Chambered Nautilus 193
Chambers Island 237
Champion, Michigan 245
Chickadee, Black-capped 24, 25, 34, 35,

    36, **37**, 70, **98**, 99, 146, 193, 219
Chief Luther Standing Bear **160**
Chinese Lantern 226
Chipmunk 113, 132
Chipmunk, Eastern 70, 71, **72**, 73, 111
Chipmunk, Gray Eastern 73
Chipmunk, Least 71, 73
Chipmunk, Ohio 73
Chipmunk, Peninsula 73
Christmas 121
Churchill River 38
Cicada 156, 158, 159
Cicada, Annual **157**
Cladina mitis 54
Cladina rangiferina 54
Cladonia cristatella 52
Clematis 95
Cmejla, Frank 66
Coccothraustes vespertinus 242
Coleridge, Samuel Taylor 26
Columbine 95, 118
Columbus, Christopher 194
Concordia Publishing House 31
Coneflower, Purple 138, 226
Connecticut 29
Coralbell 118
Cottontail 12, 13, 17
Cottonwood, Black 39
Cottonwood, Eastern 39, 181
Country Today, The - Foreword
Cowberry 208
Cowbird, Brown-headed 102, 173
Cranberry 205, **207**, 208
Cranberry, American 208
Cranberry, Highbush 227
Cranberry, Large 208
Cranberry, Mountain 208
Cranberry, Northern 206
Cranberry, Small-fruited 206
Cranberry, Wild 121
Crane, Sandhill 78, 119
Cricket, Field 171
Crow, American **56**, 57, 59, 75
Crowfoot Family 95
Cypress, Bald 196, 201

D

Daddy-long-legs 163, 164, **165**, 166
Daisy, Oxeye 193
de Kirline, L. 100
Deer, White-tailed 67, 234, **235**, 236
Delafield, Major 244
Delcarson 242
Delphinium 95
Dendrochronologist 196
Dirca palustris 82
Dogwood, Canada **107**
Doll's Eyes 176, **177**, 178
Dolomite 47
Dolostone 83, 103, 106
Door County - Foreword, Intro, 8, 47,
    67, 71, 73, 83, 121, 122, 139, 237,
    245
Door County Advocate - Intro
Door-Kewaunee Normal School -
    Intro, 30
Dove, Mourning 10, 17
Dover Publications, Inc. 5, 50
Drummond Island 71
Dryocopus pileatus 96
Duck, Common Goldeneye 75, 97
Duck, Wood 97, 202
Dutchman's Breeches 84, 92
Dutchman's Pipe 150

E

Earth Day 74
East Indies 171
Eastern Moths 126
Egypt 51
El Niño 115
Elder 178
Elder, Box 244
Elephant 105, 111
Elm, American 70, 181
Encyclopedia Brittanica 13
England 61, 135, 220
English-Eskimo Dictionary 33
Ephraim 47
Erdman, Tom 230
Europe 39, 41, 55, 93, 134, 179, 190,

192, 205, 217
Everett, David 205

F

Fairfield, Pennsylvania 239
falcon 16
Familiar Quotations 44
Farm, THE 58
Feldspar 47
Fern, Asparagus 122
Fern, Bracken 119, 121
Fern, Christmas 121
Fern, Cinnamon 121
Fern Finder 122
Fern, Green Spleenwort 121
Fern, Maidenhair **120**, 121
Fern, Rock-cap 121
Fern, Royal 121
Fern, Sensitive 121
Fibonacci, Leonardo 192
Fibonacci series 192, 193
Fibonacci spiral 193
Finland 61
Fir, Balsam 239, 241, 242
Fir twigs, Balsam **240**
Fish Creek 242
Flader, Susan L. 236
Flagg, Wilson 100
Flambeau 206
Flicker, Common 97
Florida 93, 124
Flycatcher, Great Crested 97
Fomes fomentarius 223
Footbridge School 30
Fort Sill, Oklahoma 246
Fox, Arctic 25
Fox, Gray 113
Fox, Red 113
Frog, Green 161
Frog, Johnie 206, 208
Frog, Leopard 159, **160**, 161, 162, 163
Frog, Pickerel 162
Frost Crystals **3**
Frost, Robert 30, 217, 250
fungi, woody 220
Fungus, Artist's Conk 222

Fungus, Birch Conk 223
Fungus, Bracket 220
Fungus, Hemlock Polypore 222
Fungus, Horse's Hoof 220, 223
Fungus, Partridge-tail 223
Fungus, Rainbow Conk 220
Fungus, Shelf 220, **221**
Fungus, Turkey-tail 220, 223

G

Gabbro 46
Ganoderma applanatum 222
Ganoderma tsugae 222
Garden Island 120, 194
Gaspé Peninsula 208
Gay, John 182
Gibbons, Euell 202, 205
Golden Nature Guide 126
Golden Ratio 192
Goldfinch, American 28, 219, 245
Goldthread 28
Goose, Canada 80
Gopher 73, 113, 114
Goshawk, Northern 16
Grackle, Common 58, 115
Grandfather Greybeards 163
Grange, Wallace Byron 237
Granite 47
Grape, Concord 205
Grape of Mt. Ida 208
Grass, Brome 128
Grasshopper 114, 171
Gray's Manual of Botany 92
Great Plains 114, 124
Great Pyramids 51
Grebe, Pied-billed 80
Greece 193
Green Bay - Foreword
Green Bay Press-Gazette - Intro
Green Mountains 5
Greenland 29, 46
Grosbeak, Evening
    24, 193, 242, **243**, 244, 245, 246
Grosbeak, Pine 245
Grosbeak, Rose-breasted 88, 119, 246
Grosbeak, Western Evening 244

Grouse, Ruffed
    28, 78, 80, **81**, 105, 178, 202, 227
Gulf of Mexico 18, 174
Gulf of St. Lawrence 208

H

Hackmatack 199, 200
Haen, Dick 190
Haen, Ginny 190
Hallowell, Anne C. 122
Hallowell, Barbara G. 122
Hamerstrom, Dr. Fran 245
Hamerstrom, Fran 18
Harrier, Northern 17, 113
Harris, Chandler - Intro
Harvestmen 163
Hasenjager, Donald 7
Hawk, Cooper's 16
Hawk, Red-tailed 17, 113
Hawk, Rough-legged 17
Hawk, Sharp-shinned 16, 17, **19**, 35
Haymaker 163
Hemlock, Eastern 67, 250
Hemlock, Poison 153
Hepatica
    44, 82, 83, 84, 92, 93, **94**, 95
Hepatica acutiloba **65**
Hepatica americana 93
Hepatica angulosa 93
Heron, Green **23**
Hidden Brook **233**
Hlinak, "Tam" 200
Hoarfrost 4, **32**
Hollyhock 118
Honesty 226
Hornbeam, American 49
Horntail 97
Hornworm, Tomato 124
Hotz, Lou 173
Hotz, Ray 173
Hummingbird, Anna's 116
Hummingbird, Ruby-throated 25, 52, 115,
    116, **117**, 118, **172**, 173, 174, 175
Humphreys, W. J. 5
Hungary 93

I

Ice-clad shoreline **253**
Iceland 29
Idaho 201
Indian, Ojibwe 28, 38, 89, 206, 238
Indian Pipe 150, **151**, 152
Indian, Woodland 194
Italy 41, 153

J

Jack-in-the-pulpit 88, 92
Jacksonport 7
Jay, Blue 20, 202
Jericho, Vermont 4, 31, 33
Jonsson, Ingrid 61
Jordan, Michael 136
Junco 226
Junco, Dark-eyed 10
Juneberry 175

K

Kacer, Walter 29
Kangaroo Lake 173, 174
Keewaydenoquay 194
Kestrel, American 6, 17
Kewaunee -
        Intro, 15, 29, 30, 185, 218, 219, 248
Kewaunee County 73, 237
Kewaunee Highway Department 47
Kewaunee River 140, 185, 219
Kieweg, Anton 219
Kieweg's Park 219
Killdeer 103, **104**, 105, 106, 130
Kingbird, Eastern 6, 219
Kotyza, Tony 185
kryllos 13

L

La Brea tar pits 244
La Chouette Des Granges De L'est 229
Labrador Tea 121
Lake Champlain 5, 33
Lake Geneva 248

Lake Huron 71, 196
Lake Michigan -
        Intro, 4, 82, 120, 194, 197
Lake Superior 244
Lake Winnipeg 201
Larch, European 199
Larch Sawfly 200
Larch, Western 199, 201
Larix laricina 200
Larix occidentalis 201
Larix sibirica 200
Larson, Professor Douglas 194, 196
Lawrence University 50
Leatherleaf 121
Leatherwood 38, 82, 83
Leek, Wild 84
Leelanau County 197
lepidopterist 63
Leyse Aluminum Factory 218
Lichen, Anaptychia 52
Lichen, British Red Soldier 52
Lichen, Old Man's Beard **53**, 55
Lichen, Parmelia 52
Lichen, Pixie Cup 52
Lichen, Reindeer Moss 52, 54
Lichen, Usnea 55
Lichterman, Roxi 140
Lily, Trout 88, 92
Limestone 47, 83
Linden Tree 132, 134, 135, 193
Lingonberry 208
Linnaeus 155, 178
Little Lake 80
Liverleaf 93
Locust, 17-year 158
London, England 61, 62
Longfellow, Henry Wadsworth 34
Los Angeles 244
Louisiana 244
Lowell, James Russell 26
Lukes, Adolph 145
Lukes, Ivan 2
Lukes, Leo 2
Lukes, Richard 2
Lukes, Uncle Joseph 190
Lunaria annua 226

M

Mackenzie, Canada 200
Mackenzie River 38, 136
Mackinac Bridge 120
Madden, Mike 71
Madison - Intro, 248
Madison Boy Scouts 130
Madison School Forest - Intro
Maine 29
Manitoba, Canada 38, 93
Manitowoc County 73, 237
Mantid, Carolina 215
Mantid, Chinese 215
Mantid, European 212, 215
Mantis, European Praying **213**
Mantis, Praying 170, 212, 214
Mantis religiosa 212
Maple, Ash-leafed 244
Maple, Manitoba 244
Maple, Sugar
        66, 68, **69**, 70, 173, 179, 250
Marigold, Marsh 92, 95
Marinette County 73
Martin, Jacqueline Briggs 31
Mayapple 93
Mayflower 92
Mayflower, Canada 93
Meadow-Rue 93, 95
Meadowlark, Eastern 6
Merganser, Red-breasted 75
Merlin 17, 18, 20
Mexico 63, 136, 139
Mexico City, Mexico 62
Mica 47
Mice, White-footed 89
Michigan 29
Midwest 114, 161
Milkweed 224
Milkweed, Butterfly 118
Milkweed Pods **225**
Miller, Chuck 102
Milwaukee 159
Milwaukee Public Museum 139, 174
Minnesota 29, 93, 173
Mississippi 244
Mississippi River 116, 238

Money Plant 226
Monotropa uniflora 150
Montana 201
Moosewood 38, 182
Morton Gneiss-schist 46
Moss, Spanish 55, 122
Moth, Actias 124
Moth, Cecropia 124
Moth, Clearwing Hummingbird 125
Moth, Eight-spotted Forester 125
Moth, Five-spotted Hawkmoth 124
Moth, Geometer 125
Moth, Luna **123**, 124, 125
Moth, Polyphemus 124
Moth, Promethea 124
Moth, Sphinx 124
Moth, Tineid 122
Mother Earth and Father Sky **77**
Mouse, White-footed 113
Mud Lake Wildlife Area 161, 245
Muenschner, Walter Conrad 178
Mushroom, Giant Puffball 183, **184**, 185
Mushroom, Honey Cap 220, 222
Mushrooms Demystified 183

N

Nasturtium 118
Native American 28, 66, 74, 132, 194,
    202, 205, 206, 208
Native, American 30
Nature Study Guild 122
Near Horizons, the Story of an Insect
    Garden 214
Netherlands 76, 155
New World 116
New York 29, 66
Newfoundland, Canada 208
North America
    99, 122, 152, 162, 179, 229, 230, 244
North American Birds of Prey 20
Northwest Territories, Canada 38
Norway 208
Nova Scotia 93
Nuthatch, Red-breasted 25, 70, 99
Nuthatch, White-breasted 24
Nymphalic antropa 61

O

Oak, Black 204
Oak, Bur 204
Oak, Chestnut 204
Oak, Northern Red **48**, 199, 202, 204
Oak, Pin 204
Oak, Scarlet 204
Oak, Scrub 204
Oak, White 202, 204
Oconto County 73
Ohio River Valley 248
Ontario 196, 248
Opicka Valley 219
Opossum **129**, 131, 168
Oriole, Baltimore 88, 119, 219
Oshkosh 204
Outagamie County 237
Ovenbird 99, 146
Owl, Acadian 229
Owl, Barred 229, 230
Owl, Ferruginous Pygmy 230
Owl, Flammulated 230
Owl, Great-horned 79, 229, 230
Owl, Kirtland's 229
Owl, Northern Pygmy 230
Owl, Saw-whet **228**, 229, 230, 231
Owl, Screech 97
Owl, Snowy **23**, 24, 230
Owl, Sparrow 229
Owl, Spotted 196
Owl, Whiskered 230
Owl, White-fronted 229
Owl, Whitney's Elf 230

P

parhelic circle 13
Paris, France 194
Parmelia sulcata 174
Parsley 153
Parsnip, Cow 153
Parthenon 193
Partridgeberry 208
Paul's Used Book Store 248
Peninsula State Park 199
Peru 18

Peterson Field Guide 126
Peterson, Roger Tory 18
Peterson's Field Guide 18
Petunia 118
Phidias 193
Phlox 118
Picea Abies 190
Picea mariana 200
Pigeon, Passenger 61, 163
pileatus 96
Pilgrim 206
Pine, Bristlecone 51, 196
Pine, Hasenjager 7, 8
Pine, Red 50
Pine, Skyline **6**, 8
Pine, White 7, 8, 75, **77**
Piptoporus betulinus 223
Poisonous Plants of the United States 178
Polypody, Common 121
Polyporaceae 222
Polypore, Birch 220
Polypore, Thick-walled Maze 220
pome 217
Poplar, Balsam 39, **40**, 41, 49, 82, 181
Poplar, Black 39
Poplar, Lombardy 41
Poplar, White 39
Populus balsamifera 38
Populus candicans 39
Populus gileadensis 39
Populus Italica 41
Porcupine 168
Potentilla, Shrubby 135, 136
Pristophora ericksonii 200
Puccoon, Red 91

Q

Quartz 47
Queen Anne's Lace **149**, 153, **154**

R

Raccoon 202
Ragweed 227
Rangelight Residence 4
Raven, Northern 59, 119

Redpoll, Common **9**, 24, 28
Redpoll, Hoary 24
Redstart, American 99
Redwood, Coastal 68
Redwood, Dawn 201
Reindeer 54
Ridges Sanctuary - Foreword, 159, 249
Robbins, Sam - Foreword
Robert Hale Limited 214
Robin, American 83, 115, 219, 229
Rogers, Walter E. 50
Roosevelt, Theodore 241
Roy and Stone Fence **45**
Ruskin, John 34

S

St. Louis 31
Sandpiper, Upland **127**
Sault St. Marie 71
Savannah River 244
Scholz, Carl 58, 59
Schubert, Doris 15
Scotland 121
Seton, Ernest Thompson 59
Shorewood Hills School - Intro
Shrew, Short-tailed 113
Shrike, Loggerhead 100
Siberia 200
Silver Dollar 226
Siskin, Pine 28
Sister Bay 212
Sister Bay Yacht Club and Resort 212
Skala, Grandma 219
Skala, Great Grandfather 140
Skunk Cabbage 82, 83, **85**
Skunk, Striped **157**
Smith, Olga A. 50
Snake, Brown 143
Snake, Bull 143
Snake, Copperhead 142
Snake, DeKay's 143
Snake, Eastern Garter **141**, 142, 143
Snake, Fox 143
Snake, Garter 159
Snake, Grass 140
Snake, Hog-nosed 130, 131, 143

Snake, Milk 142, 143
Snake, Northern Red-bellied 143
Snake, Northern Ring-necked 143
Snake, Northern Water 142, 143
Snake, Pine 142
Snake, Smooth Green 140, 143
Snake, Water Moccasin 142
Snake, Western Fox 142
Snow Cones **43**
Snow Crystals 5
Snowbound 15
Snowflake **14**
Snowflake Bentley 5, 31
Snowflake Bentley: Man of Science, Man
    of God 31
Socrates 153
Solomon's Seal 93
South America 116, 162
Sparrow, Fox 83
Sparrow, House 24
Sparrow, Tree 24, 25, 226
Sparrow, White-crowned 115
Sparrow, White-throated
    10, 115, 147, 226
Sparrow, White-throated, in birdbath **144**
Spermophile, 13-lined
    111, **112**, 113, 114
Spider, Crab **154**
Spider, Flower **154**
Spleenwort, Green 121
Spleenwort, Maidenhair 121
Spring Beauty 92
Spruce 241
Spruce, Black 200, 201
Spruce, Norway 190, **191**, 192, 193
Spruce, Sitka 196
Spruce, White 75, 111
Sprunt Jr., Alexander 20
Squirrel Corn 92
Squirrel, Flying 97, 111
Squirrel, Gray 111
Squirrel, Ground 113, 114
Squirrel, Red 111, 231, 239
Squirrel, Thirteen-lined Ground 73
Stalking the Wild Asparagus 202, 205
Starling, European 58
Stevens Point 46
Stoddard, Gloria 31

Stone Fence **45**
Stopping By Woods On a Snowy Evening
    250
Sturgeon Bay 7, 80
sublimation 4
sundog 13
Sunflower, Mexican 226
Swan, Mute 82
Swan, Tundra 80
Sweden 61
Sycamore 50

T

Tacamahac 38, 41
Tacamahaca 41
Tam O' Shanter 88
Tamarack **198**, 200, 201, 229
Tamarack, American 199, 200
Tanager, Scarlet 88, 146
Teale, Edwin Way 12, 214, 215
Tetterwort 91
Texas 124
Thimbleberry 166, 176
Thinking Like A Mountain... 236
Thomson, Dr. John 174
Thoreau, Henry David
    75, 182, 187, 219, 250
Thornhill, Claude 31
Thrasher, Brown 146
Thrush, Hermit 83
Thrush, Wood 146
Thuja occidentalis 196
Tithonia 226
Toft, Emma 28, 34, 35, 147, 200, 246
Toft Point 35, 54, 97, 162
Tomato, Brandywine 226
Toothwort 91
Trailing Arbutus 92, 182
Trametes versicolor 223
Tree Flowers of Forest, Park and Street 50
Trillium 93
Trillium, Giant 84, 88, **90**
Trinity College 135
Trumpet Vine 118
Trypethelium virens 51, 54
Turkey, Wild **21**, 202

Turtle, Box 108, 111
Turtle, Painted **109**, 110
Turtle, Snapping 108, 110, 168

U

Umbelliferae 153
uniflora 150
United States 61, 118, 139, 153, 161, 175,
    192, 244, 246, 251
University of Guelph, Ontario, Canada
    194
University of Missouri Press 236
University of Wisconsin-Madison 174
Unter den Linden 135
usneoides 55

V

Vaccinium macrocarpon 208
Vaccinium Oxycoccos 206
Vaccinium Vitis-Idaea 208
Van Dyke, Henry 44
Vermont 4, 29, 66
Verona - Intro
Verrucaria nigrescens 51, 54
Violet 88, 93
Vireo, Red-eyed 99, 100, 102, 103
Virginia Creeper 102, 125
Vole, Meadow 111
Vulture, Turkey 83

W

Walkingstick 168, **169**, 170, 171, 212
Walnut, Black 134
Warbler, Parula 55
Warbler, Yellow-rumped 83, 226
Waupaca 242
Waupaca County 237
Wausau 244
Way to Game Abundance, The 237
Weasel, Short-tailed 113
Webster's Third International Dictionary
    200
WESA stone 46
White House 241

Whitefish Dunes State Park 67
Whittier, John Greenleaf 15
Wild Animals I Have Known 59
Winnebago County 237
Wintergreen 121
Wisconsin 16, 18, 22, 24, 25, 29, 38, 54,
    55 62, 66, 73, 115, 121, 132,
    142, 43, 170, 185, 196, 200, 229,
    236, 237, 239, 242, 245, 248
Wisconsin Conservation Dept. 237
Wisconsin Rapids 46, 209, 214
Wisconsin River 46
Wood County 209
Woodcock 128
Woodpecker, Downy 18, 24, 99, 219
Woodpecker, Hairy 17, 18, 20, 24
Woodpecker, Pileated 96, 97, **98**, 99
Woodpecker, Red-bellied 20

Y

Yellowlegs, Lesser **- Foreword**
Yeomans, Bob 195, 197
Yeomans, Charlotte 197
Young, Dr. Allen 139

Z

Zimmerman, Jim - Foreword, Intro
Zinnia 118
Zuell, Florence 140

Other Books by Roy Lukes:

Once Around The Sun, A Door County Journal, 1976
Out On A Limb, A Journal Of Wisconsin Birding, 1979
The Ridges Sanctuary, 1988
Toft Point, A Legacy Of People And Pines, 1998